World Wisdom
The Library of Perennial Philosophy

The Library of Perennial Philosophy is dedicated to the exposition of the timeless Truth underlying the diverse religions. This Truth, often referred to as the *Sophia Perennis*—or Perennial Wisdom—finds its expression in the revealed Scriptures as well as the writings of the great sages and the artistic creations of the traditional worlds.

The Play of Masks appears as one of our selections in the Writings of Frithjof Schuon series.

The Writings of Frithjof Schuon

The Writings of Frithjof Schuon form the foundation of our library because he is the pre-eminent exponent of the Perennial Philosophy. His work illuminates this perspective in both an essential and comprehensive manner like none other.

English Language Writings of Frithjof Schuon

Original Books

The Transcendent Unity of Religions
Spiritual Perspectives and Human Facts
Gnosis: Divine Wisdom
Language of the Self
Stations of Wisdom
Understanding Islam
Light on the Ancient Worlds
Treasures of Buddhism (In the Tracks of Buddhism)
Logic and Transcendence
Esoterism as Principle and as Way
Castes and Races
Sufism: Veil and Quintessence
From the Divine to the Human
Christianity/Islam: Essays on Esoteric Ecumenicism
Survey of Metaphysics and Esoterism
In the Face of the Absolute
The Feathered Sun: Plains Indians in Art and Philosophy
To Have a Center
Roots of the Human Condition
Images of Primordial and Mystic Beauty: Paintings by Frithjof Schuon
Echoes of Perennial Wisdom
The Play of Masks
Road to the Heart: Poems
The Transfiguration of Man
The Eye of the Heart
Form and Substance in the Religions
Adastra & Stella Maris: Poems by Frithjof Schuon (bilingual edition)
Autumn Leaves & The Ring: Poems by Frithjof Schuon (bilingual edition)
Songs without Names, Volumes I-VI: Poems by Frithjof Schuon
Songs without Names, Volumes VII-XII: Poems by Frithjof Schuon
World Wheel, Volumes I-III: Poems by Frithjof Schuon
World Wheel, Volumes IV-VII: Poems by Frithjof Schuon
Primordial Meditation: Contemplating the Real

Edited Writings

The Essential Frithjof Schuon, ed. Seyyed Hossein Nasr
Songs for a Spiritual Traveler: Selected Poems (bilingual edition)
René Guénon: Some Observations, ed. William Stoddart
The Fullness of God: Frithjof Schuon on Christianity, ed. James S. Cutsinger
Prayer Fashions Man: Frithjof Schuon on the Spiritual Life, ed. James S. Cutsinger
Art from the Sacred to the Profane: East and West, ed. Catherine Schuon
Splendor of the True: A Frithjof Schuon Reader, ed. James S. Cutsinger
Towards the Essential: Selected Letters of Frithjof Schuon, ed. Thierry Béguelin
Letters of Frithjof Schuon: Reflections on the Perennial Philosophy,
ed. Michael Oren Fitzgerald

The Play of Masks

A New Translation with Selected Letters

by

Frithjof Schuon

Includes Other Previously
Unpublished Writings

Edited by
Harry Oldmeadow

World Wisdom

The Play of Masks:
A New Translation with Selected Letters
© 2024 World Wisdom, Inc.

Translated by Mark Perry and Jean-Pierre Lafouge

Published in French as Le Jeu des Masques,
L'Age d'Homme, 1992

Library of Congress Cataloging-in-Publication Data

Cover:
Indian temple hanging (*pichvai*) of Krishna and the *gopīs*,
Nathdwara, Rajasthan, India, 19th century

Photograph of Frithjof Schuon on p. xi by Michael Pollack

Printed on acid-free paper in the United States of America

For information address World Wisdom, Inc.
P.O. Box 2682, Bloomington, Indiana 47402
www.worldwisdom.com

CONTENTS

EDITOR'S PREFACE

The ancient Vedic Scriptures tell of a wondrous net that hangs over the palace of the god Indra, situated on Mount Meru, the *axis mundi* of Hindu cosmology. At each vertex of this vast, glittering net is a multi-faceted jewel that reflects all the others. Each jewel is thus a kind of microcosm, containing all. This image comes to mind while reading *The Play of Masks*. Each of the author's works is like a jewel in Indra's net: in each we find the same unchanging wisdom, the *sophia perennis*, which informs all integral mythological and religious traditions. Frithjof Schuon is the pre-eminent metaphysician of our time. If it be asked—as well it might in our darkened times—"What is metaphysics?", the short answer is "the science of the Real", the Real here being properly understood as that which is immutable, infinite and eternal, that from which issues everything in the time-space world, which is nothing other than a tissue of contingencies and relativities (in the Hindu lexicon, *Māyā*).

In Schuon's many essays, ranging over manifold forms from across the globe, we find extended expositions of metaphysical doctrines, their application in the cosmological realm, and their pertinence to the spiritual life, which any metaphysical understanding necessarily entails. We sometimes find the author, Manjushri-like, brandishing "the sword of gnosis" to cut through the knots of ignorance that hold most of us captive. In some of his writings this involves an implacable critique of those anti-traditional negations and pseudo-mythologies that came to exert such a tenacious grip on the modern outlook. But there is relatively little of what we might call "clearing the decks" in *The Play of Masks*, a slender volume in which the author most often distils the quintessence of traditional wisdom without paying sustained attention to all those false and fraudulent philosophies that might hitherto have occluded our view. Schuon's purpose here is often like that of the poet: to find a simple, direct, and resonant statement of truths that by their nature always remain the same, but which are amenable to endless variegation. As he has written elsewhere, "Everything has already been said, and even well said; but it is always necessary to recall it anew, and in so doing . . . to actualize in thought the certitudes contained, not in the thinking ego, but in the transpersonal substance of the human intelligence".[1]

Whatever the subject immediately at hand, the underlying purpose of Schuon's work remains the same: the illumination and explication of the *sophia perennis* and its implications for our human vocation. This was true of his first book, his last, and all the others in between. It might be noted, moreover, that his work exhibits a unique and remarkable quality: it does not "evolve"; his early work is no less authoritative, or in any sense less complete, than the writings he produced later in life. One does not trace a trajectory, as it were. Rather, we are given so many variations on a few abiding themes considered from a variety of vantage-points and in a multitude of different contexts. The preceding remarks notwithstanding, whilst the fundamental substance of Schuon's work remained constant, his later writings are characterized by a move towards a more lyrical and poetic mode of expression, and by the intention to "essentialize" traditional teachings—that is, to some degree to free them from their dogmatic constraints, to universalize them. Religious exoterism particularizes the universal whereas integral esoterism, such as we find here, universalizes the particular. This is especially evident in *The Play of Masks*.

Following our reference to Vedic cosmology, mention may be made of the fact that from the outset, as he has several times attested, Schuon took his metaphysical bearings from the *Vedānta*, by no means the only authoritative expression of the "science of the Real"—which, in fact, is to be found at the esoteric heart of religion everywhere in the world of Tradition—but perhaps the most lucid and most adequate, though obviously no expression of the *sophia perennis* could ever be exhaustive. The reader will find in *The Play of Masks* frequent reference to the cardinal axioms and terms of the *Vedānta*: *Brahman*, *Ātmā*, *Māyā*, and so on. Perhaps as a kind of counterbalance, Schuon also draws frequently on the Christian gospels. But, as in all his works, he freely refers to all of the world's great religious and sapiential patrimonies. The author situated himself within the traditional framework of Islam, more particularly within the fold of Sufism. He has written extensively and at great depth about the Islamic tradition,

---

[1] Frithjof Schuon, *In the Face of the Absolute* (Bloomington, Indiana: World Wisdom, 1989), p. 5.

most obviously in *Understanding Islam* (first published in 1963), but in several other books also. The present volume is less concerned with the particularities of this or that tradition, and more focused on the underlying verities of the Wisdom of the Ages to which each tradition gives its own accent and coloration, and on the spiritual imperatives of metaphysical knowledge: thus the insistence that "if metaphysical knowledge remains purely mental, it is worth practically nothing; knowledge is of value only on condition that it be prolonged in both love and will" (p. 13).

There are many ways in which Schuon's perennial message might be encapsulated. When he was asked in an interview, in 1991, to summarize his philosophy, he replied: "There are four elements that are essential: There is first *discernment* between the Absolute and the relative. . . . Then, *prayer*, because if you understand what is essential and Absolute, you want to assimilate it. . . . The third thing is intrinsic *morality*, beauty of the soul. . . . The fourth dimension is *beauty*: beauty of forms."[2] The present volume opens with the following statement: "Total intelligence, free will, sentiment capable of disinterestedness: these are the prerogatives that place man at the summit of terrestrial creatures" (p. 1). These divine endowments are a kind of "celestial potentiality" (p. 16) that we only fulfil when we come "to know the True, to will the Good, to love the Beautiful" (p. 1). It will not escape the alert reader's attention that the author frequently affirms, as did Plato, the reciprocal relations and impregnable nexus between Truth, Goodness, and Beauty. He more than once cites the Platonic axiom that "Beauty is the splendor of the true" and understands virtue as "the beauty of the soul". To compress several of Schuon's "abiding themes" into a single declaration we might, then, put his message this way: we *know* the Truth, become "conscious of the Real", through that intelligence which is our human birthright; we *will* the Good through prayer and the cultivation of virtue; and we *love* Beauty as a reverberation of the Divine in the world of forms. Knowledge, Virtue, Love—the veritable touchstones of the *sophia perennis*.

* * *

[2] Quoted in Michael Fitzgerald, *Frithjof Schuon: Messenger of the Perennial Philosophy* (Bloomington, Indiana: World Wisdom, 2010), p. xx (italics added).

The Play of Masks is a late and, quantitatively speaking, a comparatively modest addition to the author's *oeuvre*, but just as the size of a jewel does not compromise its beauty or brilliance, so it is with the author's books. It first appeared in French in 1992 as *Le jeu des masques* (Lausanne: L'Age de Homme) and soon after in English translation (Bloomington, Indiana: World Wisdom). The Appendix of the present volume includes an essay, "Norms and Paradoxes in Initiatic Alchemy", which first appeared in *Sophia: The Journal of Traditional Studies*, 1:1, 1995. The reader will also find in the Appendix previously unpublished excerpts from Schuon's correspondence and other writings. The editor's notes are designed to assist the reader in understanding the author's many references and allusions to the vast treasure-house of Tradition. A glossary of foreign terms is also included.

Harry Oldmeadow

Frithjof Schuon

FOREWORD

As with most of our books, this volume is not dedicated to a highly specific subject, but represents rather a general survey; the chapters are little independent treatises that, in many cases, summarize the general doctrine. The third article of this compilation has lent its name to the whole book; coincidentally, this title is well suited to a dialectic that presents the same fundamental theses under different aspects, but which are reiterated for the sake of clarity as well as completeness.

Without a doubt, metaphysics aims in the first place at an understanding of the total Universe, which extends from the divine Order all the way to earthly contingencies—this is the reciprocity between *Ātmā* and *Māyā*—while offering, furthermore, openings that are less demanding intellectually albeit humanly crucial, and which are all the more important given that we live in a world wherein the abuse of intelligence replaces wisdom.

Even if our writings were to have on average no other result than the restitution, for a few, of this saving barque that is prayer, we would owe it to God to be deeply gratified.

Prerogatives of the Human State

Total intelligence, free will, sentiment capable of disinterestedness: these are the prerogatives that place man at the summit of terrestrial creatures. Being total, the intelligence takes cognizance of all that is, in the world of principles as well as in that of phenomena; being free, the will may choose even that which is contrary to one's immediate interest or to what is agreeable; being disinterested, sentiment is capable of looking at itself from the outside, just as it can put itself in another's place. Every man can do so in principle, whereas animals cannot, a fact which cuts short the objection that not all men are humble and charitable; no doubt, the effects of the "Fall" weaken the prerogatives of human nature, but they cannot abolish them without abolishing man himself. To say that man is endowed with a sensibility capable of objectivity means that he possesses a subjectivity not closed in on itself, but open unto others and unto Heaven; in fact, every normal man may find himself in a situation where he will spontaneously manifest the human capacity for compassion or generosity, and every man is endowed, in his substance, with what could be called the "religious instinct".

Total intelligence, free will, disinterested sentiment; and consequently: to know the True, to will the Good, to love the Beautiful. "Horizontally", the Truth concerns the cosmic, hence phenomenal, order; "vertically", it concerns the metaphysical, hence principial, order. And likewise with the Good: on the one hand, it is practical, secondary, contingent; on the other, it is spiritual, essential, absolute. Similarly again with Beauty, which at first sight is outward, in which case it is the aesthetic quality, that of virgin nature, of creatures, sacred art, traditional crafts; but with all the more reason is it inward, in which case it is the moral quality, nobility of character. According to an Islamic saying, "God is beautiful and He loves Beauty"; this means implicitly that God invites us to participate in His Nature—in the Sovereign Good—through Virtue, in the context of the Truth and the Way.

Ideally, normatively, and vocationally, man is Intelligence, Strength, and Virtue; now, it is important to consider Virtue in two aspects, one "terrestrial" and the other "celestial". Socially, it demands humility and compassion; spiritually, it consists of fear and love of God. Fear implies resignation to the divine Will; love implies trust in Mercy.

What is fear and love towards God becomes—*mutatis mutandis*—respect and good will towards the neighbor; good will as a matter of principle towards any stranger, not weakness towards someone known to be unworthy. Love implies fear, for one can love only what one respects; trust in divine Mercy and mystical intimacy with Heaven indeed allow of no casualness; this also follows from that crucial quality which is the sense of the sacred, wherein fear and love meet.

In the experience of the aesthetic and of the erotic, the ego is extinguished—or forgets itself—before a grandeur other than itself: to love a reality worthy of being loved is an attitude of objectivity that the subjective experience of fascination cannot abolish. This is to say that love has two poles, one subjective, the other objective; it is the latter that must determine the experience since it is the reason for being of the attraction. Sincere love is not a roundabout way of loving oneself; it is founded upon an object worthy of admiration, of adoration, of desire for union; and the quintessence of every love, and even of every virtue, can only be the love of God.

The complexity of our subject allows us to consider it now from another angle and to take account of other points of reference, and this at the risk of repeating ourselves, which cannot be avoided in such a matter.

Human intelligence is, virtually and vocationally, the certitude of the Absolute. The idea of the Absolute implies on the one hand that of the relative and on the other that of the relationships between the two, namely the prefiguration of the relative in the Absolute and the projection of the Absolute in the relative; the first relationship gives rise to the personal God, and the second, to the supreme Angel.[1]

---

[1] This angel is the *Metatron* of the Kabbalah, the *Rūh* of the Koran, and the *Buddhi*—or *Trimūrti*—of the *Vedānta*; it is also the Holy Spirit of Christian doctrine in its function of illuminating hearts.

Human will is, virtually and vocationally, the tendency towards the absolute Good; secondary goods, whether they be necessary or simply useful, are determined indirectly by the choice of the supreme Good. The will is instrumental, not inspirational: we know and love, not what we will, but rather we will what we know and love; it is not the will that determines our personality, it is intelligence and sentiment.[2]

Human sentiment—the soul if one wishes—is, virtually and vocationally, love of Sovereign Beauty and of its reverberations in the world and in ourselves; in the latter case, the beauties are virtues and also, on a less eminent plane, artistic gifts. "God", "myself", "others": these are three dimensions to which correspond respectively piety, humility, and charity or, we could say, the contemplative, characterial, and social qualities.

In the case of piety—which is essentially the sense of the sacred, of the transcendent, of profundity—the complementary virtues of humility and charity are directed towards the Sovereign Good and make it their object; which is to say that the quality of piety coincides in the end with holiness, which implies, *a priori*, joy through God and peace in Him. In this context, humility becomes awareness of our metaphysical nothingness, and charity becomes awareness of the divine immanence in beings and in things; to have a sense of the sacred is to be aware that all qualities or values not only proceed from the Infinite but also draw us towards it. The soul, we have said, is quintessentially love of Sovereign Beauty; from a less fundamental and more empirical point of view, we could say that the substance of the soul is the unconscious search for a lost Paradise, which in reality is "within you".

If the fundamental virtues are beauties, conversely each sensible beauty bears witness to the virtues: it is "pious"—that is "ascendant" or "essentializing"—because it manifests celestial archetypes; it is "humble" because it submits to the universal laws and, because of this, excludes all excess; and it is "charitable" in the sense that it radiates and enriches without ever asking for anything in return.

---

[2] The words "sentiment" and "sentimental" too often evoke the idea of an opposition to reason and the reasonable, which is abusive since a sentiment can be right just as a reasoning can be wrong.

Let us add that, in the human world, spirituality alone engenders beauty, without which the normal and non-perverted man cannot live.

The rigorous virtues, such as courage and incorruptibility, are on the one hand linked indirectly to the fundamental virtues, and on the other can be explained by the fact that we live in a limited and dissonant world; in Paradise, the aggressive and defensive virtues no longer have any reason for being. To fight for a just cause is to be charitable towards society; and to assert towards men an authority that belongs to us by divine right is to be humble towards God. In this way, every virtue, be it combative or adamantine, is connected directly or indirectly with the love of God, otherwise it could not be a virtue, precisely.

If piety, humility, and charity are the greatest virtues, impiety,[3] pride, egoism, and malice will be the greatest vices; this is only too obvious, but it is worth specifying, all the more so since it is sometimes less difficult to fight a concrete fault than to realize an ideal of virtue. Besides the vices, there are also the caricatures of virtue, which being stupid or hypocritical are vicious in their turn: given that impiety, pride, and egoism are defects, it does not follow that false piety, false humility, and false charity are qualities. Unquestionably, goodness is integral only on condition of being combined with strength.[4]

Alongside virtue as spontaneous beauty of soul, there is also the effort towards virtue; both things are combined in most cases. Doubtless, an attitude or a behavior that one must force oneself to practice is not yet an established virtue, even though it is already a kind of virtue if the intention is sincere.

[3] By impiety we mean, not the mere fact of not believing in God, but the fundamental tendency not to believe in Him; herein lies the whole difference between the "accident" and "substance".

[4] A Russian monk told us that Jesus treated the Temple merchants harshly in order to show that He was capable of exercising violence—an opinion which, when properly understood, is not lacking in pertinence, despite its paradoxical and discordant aspect.

Our personality is founded upon that which we know to be real, and consequently also, but in a negative sense, upon that which we know to be unreal, or less real.

Similarly, our personality is founded upon that which we will, namely a given good and with all the more reason the good as such, and consequently also upon that which we reject, namely a given evil and *a fortiori* evil as such.

Similarly again, our personality is founded upon that which we love, namely beauty—be it physical, moral, or archetypal—and consequently also, in a negative sense, upon that which we detest, namely ugliness in all its aspects. A remark may be called for here: clearly, the beauty of a morally ugly person obliges us neither to love this person because of their beauty, nor to deny this beauty because of their moral ugliness; inversely, the ugliness of a morally beautiful person obliges us neither to detest this person because of their ugliness, nor to deny this ugliness because of their moral beauty. Confusions of this kind frequently occur on planes more subtle than the one at issue here, so that it is worth taking the trouble to point out these kinds of misconceptions.

Beauty is substance, and ugliness accident; the relationship is the same between love and hate; it is the relationship between good and evil in an altogether general sense. The world is fundamentally made of beauty, not ugliness, and the soul is made of love, not hatred; the world could not contain any ugliness if it did not contain *a priori* far more beauty;[5] and it is only the greatness of our love that entitles us to aversion.

To discern the real is also to discern the unreal, or the less real, the contingent, the relative; to will the good is by that very fact to reject evil; to love the beautiful is *ipso facto* to detest the ugly, be it only through absence of love or through indifference. For we find ourselves in a world woven of imperfections, which obliges us to perceive its limitations and dissonances and to reject or combat them if need be.

---

[5] At least in normal circumstances, which predominate by far over the exceptional conditions of the "Iron Age".

We could also say that intelligence, according to whether it is applied to the Absolute or the contingent, to the Real or the illusory, is either unitive or separative: if unitive, it assimilates; if separative, it eliminates. Nevertheless, the essence of intelligence can only be union, namely synthesis, not analysis; or contemplation, not discrimination.

Likewise, the will, according to whether it seeks the good or opposes evil, is either positive or negative, leaving aside the human possibility of inverting the normal order of things: if positive, the will is constructive, it realizes or creates; if negative, it rejects or destroys. But the essence of the will is the choice of the good and the realization of this choice; all secondary inclinations derive from this according to the circumstantial contingencies imposed by the here-below, and which could not exist close to God.

Likewise again, sentiment, according to whether it reacts to the true or the false, to good or evil, to the beautiful or the ugly—and this apart from the question of knowing whether or not the reaction is appropriate—is either attraction or aversion, either love or hatred: the desire for union or on the contrary, the desire to turn away. The essence of sentiment is nonetheless love, because the essence of the Real is beauty, goodness, beatitude.

Hatred, when it is directed against people or against good things, harms humility and charity as much as it does piety; scorn, however, may be a self-defensive reflex; if physical disgust is permissible, moral disgust is so with all the more reason. Passional hatred also injures intelligence since it violates truth; it is not for nothing that one speaks of "blind hatred". But there is a hatred that on the contrary is lucid and thus has nothing passional about it, and this is the aversion to our own faults and to what corresponds to them in the world around us.

Intelligence should operate on the basis of an assessment, and not out of a sentimental reaction; the will, by contrast, may operate in both ways, provided the option be appropriate. To ask what the purpose of sentiment is, is to ask what the purpose of love is: now, like knowledge, love seeks union, with the difference that in the first case the union is intellective and in the second, affective; in Hindu terms, this is the difference between *jnāna* and *bhakti*.

In a world largely under the influence of the centrifugal principle—the *princeps hujus mundi*—union and love cannot avoid being accompanied by a negative mode; ambiguity enters into the very definition of *Māyā*, the Absolute alone being beyond oppositions. Thus, there is no contradiction in the fact that sentiment, while coinciding substantially with love, nonetheless implies the possibility of aversion.

To be beyond oppositions means: beyond modes and accidents, such as activity and passivity, the dynamic and the static, hot and cold, white and black; or beyond opposite excesses, such as agitation and indolence, or violence and weakness; but it cannot mean: beyond the true and the false, or good and evil, for in these cases the second term is a privation of being, as it were, and not a mode of manifestation.

—— .:. ——

A metaphysical digression might be relevant here. To the attestation that "*Brahman* is Reality" (*Brahma satyam*) is joined the affirmation that "the world is merely appearance" (*jagan mithyā*); similarly—in an altogether different traditional climate—the axiom that "God alone is" (*illā 'Llāh*) requires as its negative complement the idea that "there is no other divinity" (*lā ilāha*). But this negation is compensated, on its own ground as it were, by the basically immanentist affirmation that "Muhammad is the Messenger of God" (*Muhammadun rasūlu 'Llāh*), which in the present context means that "the Perfect is the emanation of the Principle"; in an analogous way, the Vedantic idea that "the world is merely appearance" is compensated by its positive complement, the idea that "the soul is not different from *Brahman*" (*jivo brahmaiva nāparah*).

In the doctrinal message of Islam as well as in the Hindu message, the affirmation of transcendence becomes extrinsically clearer by means of a relativizing negative affirmation, which in its turn is surpassed by a compensatory affirmation of immanence. According to transcendence, we are supposed to love only the Sovereign Good, to which our power of love is proportioned since we are men; according to immanence, "it is not for the love of the spouse that the spouse is dear, but for the love of *Ātmā* which is in him".

When speaking of specifically human intelligence, one can proceed from the notions of transcendence and immanence; in other words, the essential question is that of knowing, on the one hand, what the loftiest content of the spirit is, and on the other, what its deepest substance is. The answer is furnished—in a Western setting—by the Eckhartian concepts of the supra-ontological, hence

7

transpersonal, "Divinity" (*Gottheit*) and the "uncreated Intellect" (*aliquid . . . increatum et increabile*). From this may be deduced the following definition: integral and primordial man is the Intellect and the consciousness of the Absolute. Or again: man is faith and the idea of God; immanent Holy Spirit on the one hand, and transcendent Truth on the other.

—— ⋮ ——

According to an initial and synthetic logic, we would say that the intelligence aims at the true, the will at the good, and love at the beautiful. But in order to ward off certain objections, we must specify that the intelligence is made to know all that is knowable and consequently has as its object also the good and the beautiful and not only the true; similarly, the will aims at all that deserves to be willed, thus also at the beautiful and the true; love in its turn aims at all that is lovable, thus also at the true and the good. In other words: from the standpoint of intelligence, the good and the beautiful are quite clearly truths, or let us say realities; from the standpoint of the will, the truth and beauty are goods; and from the standpoint of love, the truth and the good have their beauty, which is much more than a manner of speaking.

—— ⋮ ——

Intelligence and will when taken together constitute what we may call the "capability" of the individual, whatever his moral and aesthetic sensibility may be.

Similarly, sensibility and will when taken together constitute the "character" of the individual, whatever his intelligence may be.

And again, intelligence and sensibility when taken together constitute the "scope" of the individual, whatever his strength of will may be.

Thus, administrative aptitude, organizational skill, and strategy pertain to the psychological dimension we call "capability", rather than to intelligence or will alone; courage and incorruptibility pertain to "character" rather than to will or sensibility alone; the powerful profundity of great poets pertains to "scope", not to sensibility or intelligence alone. All these gifts have a conditional, not unconditional, value: in Paradise one no longer has need of skill, because there is no longer anything to organize; neither does one need courage, because there is no longer any evil to combat; and one no longer has need of genius, because there is no longer anything to invent or produce. However, one cannot do without the essential virtues—piety, humility, and charity—for they pertain to the very nature of the Sovereign Good, which is to say that they are part of our being.

Truth, Way, and Virtue: Virtue is the touchstone of our sincerity; without it, Truth does not belong to us and the Way eludes us.[6] The Truth is what we must know; the Way is what we must do; Virtue is what we must love, become, and be. The sufficient reason for the three fundamental perfections of man is the consciousness of the Absolute; without the possibility of this consciousness, the prerogatives of the human state could not be explained.

Truth, Way, Virtue; in other words: doctrine, method, qualification; discriminative and contemplative intelligence, realizatory will, at once forceful and persevering, and soul capable of objectivity, hence of disinterestedness, compassion, generosity. From the more particular point of view of spiritual alchemy it could be said: meditative comprehension, operative concentration, psychic conformity; this third element means that enlightening comprehension and transforming concentration require a climate of moral beauty. Whosoever says beauty, says goodness and happiness, or beatitude; this allows us to paraphrase the well-known Platonic formula thus: "Goodness—and along with it beatitude—is the splendor of the true."

Besides his objective intelligence, free will, and capacity for disinterestedness, the human being is distinguished by thought and language, and as to his bodily form, the vertical position; memory, imagination, and intuition he shares in common with animals. Reason, however, belongs to man alone; we say reason and not intelligence, for on the one hand intelligence cannot be reduced to reason, and on the other, it

[6] "Though I speak with the tongues of men and of angels, and have not charity, I am become as sounding brass, or a tinkling cymbal" (I Cor. 13:1).

is also to be found in the animal kingdom. Incontestably, animals also possess will and sentiment; the difference between them and men is both absolute and relative: it is absolute with respect to the specifically human prerogatives, and relative with respect to the faculties as such.

As for reason, theologians rightly consider that it is a sort of infirmity due to the "Fall" of Adam, and that the angels do not possess it since they enjoy the direct perception of principles, causes, and effects. Nonetheless, reason has to have a positive aspect, in the sense that it is inseparable from language and that it can coexist with angelic intuition, or—what amounts to the same thing—with intellectual intuition, or pure intellection. As for articulated thought, even the angels have to be able to make use of the rational faculty, otherwise there would be no sacred Scriptures. All in all, reason becomes an infirmity only in the case of abusive speculation by the ignoramus who pretends to knowledge. An angel or a sage can certainly be rational, but never rationalistic; he need not "conclude" when he can "perceive", but he may explain an intellective perception with the aid of a dialectic which is perforce that of the logician.

The fact that the animals, like the angels, have intuition but not reason, gives rise to the curious phenomenon of zoolatry, all the more as horizontal intuition is often more developed in animals than in men, so that they appear like the traces of celestial archetypes, or like their "mediums" so to speak. It is worth noting that there are animals sensitive to spiritual influences, to the point of being able to vehicle them, becoming thus receptacles of *barakah*.

An essential trait distinguishing man from the animals is that man knows he must die, whereas the animals do not. Now this knowledge of death is a proof of immortality; it is only because man is immortal that his faculties enable him to note the fact of his earthly impermanence. To speak of the consciousness of death is to speak of the religious phenomenon; and let us specify that this phenomenon is a part of ecology in the total sense of the term; for without religion—or without authentic religion—a human collectivity cannot survive in the long run; that is to say, it cannot remain human.

— .:. —

The human being, when defined or described according to the principle of duality, is divided into an outward man and an inward man—one being sensorial-cerebral and terrestrial, and the other intellective-cardiac and celestial. When defined according to the principle of trinity, man is divided into intelligence, will, and sentiment; according to the principle of quaternity, he will be composed of reason, intuition, memory, and imagination; these constitute so to speak two axes, one "vertical" and the other "horizontal".

Now it is the principle of trinity that takes precedence, in the sense that it is the happy medium between synthesis and analysis: it is more explicit than duality and more essential than quaternity; being closer to unity than the even numbers, trinity reflects more directly Being itself.

—— .¦. ——

Supreme Reality equals Sovereign Good.

Being absolute, the Supreme Reality is infinite; the same is true of the Sovereign Good, which is absolute Reality conceived of in terms of its nature or its content.

In the world, every reality as such bears witness to the Supreme Reality, to Reality in itself. And similarly, every good as such bears witness to the Sovereign Good, to the Good in itself.

Human intelligence, or the intellect, cannot disclose to us the self-hood of the Absolute, and no sensible person would ask this of it; the intellect can provide us points of reference, and this is all that is necessary as regards discriminative and introductory knowledge, namely the knowledge that can be expressed through words. But the intellect is not only discriminative, it is also contemplative, hence unitive, and in this respect it cannot be said to be limited, any more than a mirror limits the light that is reflected in it; the contemplative dimension of the intellect coincides with the ineffable.[7]

---

[7] A pernicious error that must be pointed out here, one which seems to be axiomatic with the false gurus of East and West, is what could be designated by the term "realizationism": it is claimed that only "realization" counts and that "theory" is nothing, as if man were not a thinking being, and as if he could undertake anything whatsoever without knowing where he was going. False masters speak readily of "developing latent energies"; now one can go to hell with all the developments and all the energies

11

It is often argued, in a theological climate, that the human intellect is too weak to know God; now the reason for being of the intellect is precisely this knowledge, indirect and indicative in a certain respect, and direct and unitive in another. An incontrovertible proof of God is that the human spirit is capable of objectivity and transcendence, transcendence being the sufficient reason of objectivity. This is not to say that such a proof is necessary to knowledge, but that it is in the nature of things and that it corroborates *ab extra* what the intellect perceives *ab intra*, given that metaphysical certitude has its roots in what we are.

Each of the prerogatives of the human state, being in its own way a cosmos, comprises two poles, an active and a passive, or a dynamic and a static. Thus, for intelligence there are discernment and contemplation, analysis and synthesis, or again, in a more subjective and empirical sense, certitude and serenity; in the will, there is the distinction between decision and perseverance, initiative and stability; and in the soul, or sentiment, between fervor and faithfulness.

Certitude and serenity, or faith and peace: peace emanates from faith, just as the Infinite—or All-Possibility—prolongs in a way the Absolute. To live, man needs peace; now, it is vain to seek this peace outside metaphysical and eschatological certitudes, to which our spirit is proportioned because it is human, and which it must assimilate because, precisely, it is proportioned to them. One would like to say with Saint Bernard, but in paraphrasing him: "O *beata certitudo, o certa beatitudo!*"[8]

one pleases; it is in any case better to die with a good theory than with a false "realization". What pseudo-spiritualists lose sight of all too easily is that, according to the maxim of the maharajahs of Benares, "There is no right superior to that of the truth."

[8] "Certitude" in place of "solitude". Solitude in God has nothing privative about it, given the Infinitude of the Sovereign Good; man is "alone" because God is "one", but this Unity is Totality.

To recapitulate: the prerogatives of the human state consist essentially of intelligence, will, and sentiment capable of objectivity and transcendence. Objectivity is the "horizontal" dimension: it is the capacity to know, to will, and to love things as they are, thus without any subjectivistic deformation; while transcendence is the "vertical" dimension: it is the capacity to know, to will, and to love God and, *ipso facto*, all the precious things that lie beyond our earthly experience and which relate more or less directly to the divine Order.

But by no means are these capacities actualized in every human being. To begin with, too many men have no metaphysical knowledge; then, too many men, if they do have it, do not know how to make it enter into their will and their love, and this cleavage between thought and the individual soul is something even much more serious than lack of knowledge. In fact, if metaphysical knowledge remains purely mental, it is worth practically nothing; knowledge is of value only on condition that it be prolonged in both love and will. Consequently, the goal of the way is first of all to mend this hereditary break, and then—on that foundation—to bring about an ascension towards the Sovereign Good which, in virtue of the mystery of immanence, is our own true Being.

Man is made of objectivity and transcendence; having forgotten this—existentially even more than mentally—his quasi-ontological vocation is to "become again what he is", which means, to return to his celestial potentiality. Without objectivity and transcendence there cannot be man, there is only the human animal; to find man, one must aspire to God.

Man in the Cosmogonic Projection

The creative radiation coincides with the mystery of existential *Māyā*—that is, not with *Māyā* as such, which at its summit includes the existentiating Principle. The entire world is *Māyā*, but *Māyā* is not entirely the world; the divine Essence, "Beyond-Being", reverberates in Relativity, giving rise to the divine Person, to creative "Being".[1]

The question of the "why" of creation has given rise to many speculations. We have answered these more than once during the course of our expositions: the cosmogonic projection has as its ultimate cause the infinitude proper to the Absolute; now, to speak of infinitude is to speak of All-Possibility and consequently the overflowing of the divine potentialities, in conformity with the principle that the Good tends towards communicating itself. It is said that God "created" the world by "a free act of His will", but this is only to emphasize that God does not act under constraint; this last term, however, lends itself to confusion for it goes without saying that God is indeed "obliged" to be faithful to His nature and for that reason cannot but manifest Himself by a quasi-eternal—or co-eternal—chain of creations,[2] a chain that, pertaining to the cosmic *Māyā*, could not affect the transcendence of Divinity, not even that of the personal Divinity.

The productions of the creative radiation are both successive and simultaneous: they are successive inasmuch as they construct the world or emerge into its space, and they are simultaneous inasmuch as, the world being now unfolded, they constitute its hierarchic structure. Universal projection does not imply any "emanation" in the literal and conventional sense of the term, and in any case it excludes all transformist evolution, even though superficial adaptations to a given environment are always possible. We refer here to principles that by their nature elude empirical investigations but not pure intellection, intellectual intuition being rooted in the very substance of the human spirit, without which *homo* would not be *sapiens*.

---

[1] This is to say that the personal God pertains to *Māyā*, of which He is the center or the summit, otherwise He could not be an interlocutor for man.

[2] As is taught notably by the Hindus and the Greeks. Metaphysical necessity is not constraint any more than liberty is arbitrariness.

—— .:. ——

At first sight, it might be thought that the conclusion of the cosmogonic projection is matter, which in fact appears as the "end point"
of the existentiating trajectory; but it is so only in a certain respect,
that of the cosmic Substance of which it is the most exteriorized and
contingent mode; it is such at least for our sensorial world, for one can
conceive of indefinitely more "solidified" substances than the matter
pertaining to our spatial cosmos.[3]

From an altogether different standpoint, we would say that the
conclusion of the manifesting trajectory is not a given substance-con-
tainer but the form-content, namely the thing created, the more or
less distant reflection of a given divine archetype. The reflections of
the "ideas" encompass not only positive phenomena but also negative
phenomena, inasmuch as these comprise positive elements on pain
of not being able to exist; a bad creature possesses at least, and necessarily, the gift of existence and in addition given qualities or given
faculties. Seen from this point of view, cosmic manifestation is overall
a good because it represents the qualities of Being.

Another mode of cosmic projection is what could be termed the
"privative accident": this projection accounts directly for the movement away from the divine Source. Manifestation is not the Principle,
the effect is not the cause; that which is "other than God" could not
possess the perfections of God; hence, in the final analysis and within
the general imperfection of the created, there results that privative and
subversive phenomenon termed evil. This is to say that the cosmogonic
ray, by plunging as it were into "nothingness", ends by manifesting "the
possibility of the impossible"; the "absurd" cannot but be produced
somewhere in the economy of the divine Possibility, otherwise the Infinite would not be the Infinite. But, strictly speaking, evil or the devil
cannot oppose the Divinity, who has no opposite; it opposes man, who
is the mirror of God and the movement towards the divine.

A mode that compensates and in a certain sense overcomes the
phenomenon of evil, and which even crowns all the other modes, is

---

[3] For the evolutionists, this matter is the stage itself—or initial substance—of universal
Possibility; gratuitous notions, such as that of the "biosphere" or "noosphere", add
nothing to attenuate this error, the effects of which are incalculable.

"reintegration": the cosmogonic movement is not merely centrifugal, it becomes centripetal in the final analysis, which is to say that it is circular; the circle of *Māyā* closes in the heart of deified man. In this respect the end result of the cosmogonic projection is man, or more specifically, the intellect perceiving the Absolute, and then the will drawing the consequences from this perception. To the question of knowing why man has been placed in the world when his fundamental vocation is to leave it, we would reply: it is precisely in order that there be someone who returns to God; this is to say that All-Possibility requires that God not only project Himself, but also realize the liberating beatitude of the return. Just as a mirror realizes in its way the sun that is reflected therein, so man realizes his divine Model: firstly by his theomorphic nature and then by the consequences that it implies.

In addition to this mode of cosmic projection that is the human phenomenon, there is so to speak a secondary but intrinsically central mode, namely the avataric mode, the "divine descent", the "incarnation"—supreme mode of the projection of *Ātmā-Māyā*. In the framework of fallen humanity, and owing to this fall, the initial human projection is repeated by the *Avatāra* in order to reestablish equilibrium and to restore to man his first vocation; it is to this that the symbolism of the dance of the *gopīs* around Krishna testifies.

—— .:. ——

Animality can manifest modes of fall as well as modes of perfection, but the animal species cannot fall; only man, participating in the divine liberty and created in order to freely choose God, can make a bad use of his freedom under the influence of that cosmic mode that is evil. Whatever the case—if we may use a somewhat unusual symbolism—just as the boomerang by its very form is destined to return to him who has thrown it, so man is predestined by his form to return to his divine prototype; whether he likes it or not, man is "condemned" to transcendence.

Humanly speaking, the privative and subversive cosmic ray is none other than the *princeps hujus mundi*; the worst of perversions is that of man because *corruptio optimi pessima*. The "dark" and "descending" tendency not only moves away from the Sovereign Good, but also rises up against it, whence the equation between the devil and pride.

17

And this permits us to insert here the following consideration: very close to pride are doubt, bitterness, and despair; the great evil for man is not only to move away from God, it is also to doubt in His Mercy. It is not to know that at the very depths of the abyss the lifeline is always there: the divine Hand is held out, provided we have the humility and the faith that allow us to grasp it. The cosmic projection moves away from God, but this movement can have nothing absolute about it; the Center is present everywhere.

It is in the nature of evil to insinuate itself in all the different orders to the extent possible: certainly, every creature has the right to live in the ambience that nature has assigned to it, but in man this right gives rise to the vices of outwardness, superficiality, worldliness, in short, to naive and irresponsible "horizontality". Yet the pitfall is not only in the tempting ambience, it is already in the human condition as such, namely in the abuse of intelligence: this can be characterized by the terms titanism, icarism, babelism, scientism, and civilizationism. Moreover, there is no excess that does not have its indirect source in some truth or reality: thus nihilism and despair could refer, quite improperly, to the universal illusion; or let us say to the cosmogonic projection's aspect of illusion. In an inversely analogous manner, the aspect of identity that reduces—or leads back—*Māyā* to *Ātmā* gives rise indirectly and caricaturally to the self-worship of certain pseudo-Vedantists, and also to idolatry in general; the image is mistaken for the real thing, the empirical "I" for the immanent Self, the psychic for the spiritual; *quod absit*.

Man, we have said, has been placed in the world so that there be in it someone who can return to God. This is what is suggested, among other signs, by that "supernaturally natural" theophany which is the human body: man being *imago Dei*, his body necessarily symbolizes a liberating return to the divine origin and in this sense it is a "remembrance of God". It is true that a noble animal—such as the stag, the lion, the eagle, the swan—also expresses a given aspect of the divine majesty, but it does not manifest the liberating return of the form to the essence; it remains in the form, whence its "horizontality". The human body, on the contrary, is "vertical"; it is a sacrament, whether it

be masculine or feminine; the difference of the sexes marks a complementarity of mode and not, quite obviously, a divergence of principle.
Sacred nudity—in India, for example—expresses the exteriorization
of that which is most interior and correlatively the interiorization of
that which is most exterior; "and that is why, naked, I dance", as Lalla
Yogishwari said upon realizing the immanent Self. Extremes meet; the
natural form can convey the supernatural essence, and the latter can
be manifested by the former.

Mentalities having little familiarity with how symbolism operates
might contest the physical deiformity of man by arguing, for example,
that God has neither an "anterior" nor a "posterior" side, and that He
could not "walk" since He is immutable; this is obvious when one
takes things literally, but it is important to understand that the incom-
mensurable levels of the points of comparison do not abolish analogy,
nor consequently symbolism.[4] The "posterior" side that may be considered here, is none other than *Māyā* inasmuch as it separates Being from
Beyond-Being; the "anterior" side is Being inasmuch as it conceives
the possibilities to be projected into the space of *Māyā*; and God's
"walk" is that very projection. Being, since it pertains to *Māyā*, "turns
its back" on Beyond-Being while remaining united with it in respect
of essence; and it "turns its face" towards *Māyā* by the very fact that
it existentiates the potentialities that will make up the world. Finally,
we would say that the Creator's "striding" is "noble": it possesses the
quality of beauty in the sense that in manifesting the archetypes God
always observes the hierarchy of things; but it goes without saying that
the Supreme Principle cannot go outside of itself. The "divine walk"
in and by *Māyā* is, so to speak, a "dream" of the Divinity, who always
remains unique and immutable; it is only for the creatures that this
dream is an exteriorization, a *creatio ex nihilo* precisely.[5]

---

[4] Furthermore, regarding our deiformity, we would point out—strange as it may
seem—that anatomy is independent of biological rigors and impurities, which, for
their part, pertain to the cosmic level and not to the archetype; they are "perversions"
due to our "fall" into post-paradisal matter, and reflect archetypal hence heavenly
functions in a privative mode.

[5] "*Brahman* is reality, the world is appearance." Let it be noted that the Vedantists do
not insist in an exclusive manner on the negative aspect of illusion; it is important in
fact to combine the idea of unreality with that of relative reality. "Mirage" is not synonymous with "nothingness"; the apparently absurd notion of a "relative nothingness"
is as fundamental as that of a "relatively absolute".

There is no virtue that does not derive from God, and there is none that He does not possess; this allows raising the question of knowing whether He possesses the virtue of humility, which by definition pertains to the creature; a question that is paradoxical and ill-sounding, to say the least, but logically inevitable. The answer is that the personal God, quite clearly, is in no way opposed to the supra-personal Divinity of which He existentiates certain potentialities; Being could not contradict Beyond-Being. The God-Person is so to speak "subject" to his own Essence, the "pure Absolute";[6] the divine Unity—or the homogeneity of the divine Order—is not impaired by the degrees of reality. To say that God is "one" does not mean that principial Reality does not comprise degrees, but that Being is unique and indivisible; it nonetheless possesses qualities and faculties, lacking which creatures would not possess them. But let us return to the question of humility: just as the personal God is "subject", hence in a certain sense "humble", in relation to the supra-personal Divinity, so too man ought to show humility in relation to his own Heart-Intellect, the immanent divine spark; the proud man sins against his own immortal essence as well as against God and men.

With all these considerations—not everyday notions, no doubt, but all the more instructive in some respects—we intend to show that universal correspondences are not limited to fundamental images but also include the secondary aspects of key-symbols.[7] In any case, and despite all the evident analogies between the celestial and terrestrial orders, it must be clearly understood that with respect to incommensurability there is nothing in the world that resembles God.

---

[6] This expression is not a tautology since we have in view the presence of *Māyā* in the divine Order.

[7] The Platonic ideas have been blamed for accounting only for certain phenomena and for excluding others, and above all for excluding the contingent aspects of things; an unfair reproach, for every phenomenal possibility, as regards what is essential in it, allows itself to be connected to an archetypal root, otherwise there would be phenomena independent of any principle.

When it is affirmed that "God is beyond the opposition between good and evil"[8] this does not mean that for God evil does not exist as such, but that God sees things under all the aspects involving them and that consequently evil for God is only a fragmentary, provisional, and wholly extrinsic aspect of a good that compensates and ultimately annuls it. In other words, God perceives evil only in its metaphysically indispensable context: in connection, on the one hand, with the good that the evil contradicts and thereby enhances, and on the other hand with the good that will overcome it because *vincit omnia Veritas*.

It has been said, in the Sufic universe, that God has no need to love and that moreover He has no need of our love; this is ill-sounding owing to the ambiguity of the term "God", a term applying *a priori* to the personified Divinity, while in the above-mentioned opinion what is in question is the supra-personal Divinity, quite obviously, which precisely is not an interlocutor for man. That Beyond-Being is the essence of love makes no difference, given that in absolute Reality love has no object outside of itself; in other words, the bipolarity subject-object is transcended in Beatitude. Let us specify that for Beyond-Being we do not exist; it is only "as Being" that the Absolute conceives our existence.[9]

We have said that God perceives evil only in its indispensable metaphysical context; this "divine perspective"—if such an expression be permissible—must be repeated in the human soul, and is even the first condition for the "way of return" we have spoken of before. Far from enclosing himself in a "horizontal" perspective and considering things in isolation and as if they were absolute, "ascending" man never loses sight of that "categorically imperative" point of reference which is God: he sees things in their divine context, not by an accidental effort but by a profound disposition of the heart. This results, for man, in all the qualities that give meaning to life: humility and charity, that is to say self-knowledge and compassion towards others; resignation to the will of Heaven and trust in Mercy, or fear and love.

[8] Such formulations are found above all in Muslim authors, always concerned with safeguarding at any price the unity of the divine Will, which theological anthropomorphism sometimes makes difficult.

[9] The great pitfall of the monotheistic theologies is the *de facto* confusion between the two levels. There is no "God" that in one and the same respect is Being and Beyond-Being, Person and Essence, *Gott* and *Gottheit*, *Īshvara* and *Paramātmā*; a personal will is one thing, All-Possibility is another.

Or again: discernment of the absolutely Real logically entails discernment of the relatively real, namely also of the ego, whence the virtue of humility; similarly, union with the divine Self entails union with our neighbor and this is the virtue of charity.[10] In this way humility and charity—rightly understood and applied—are criteria of sincerity for metaphysical discernment on the one hand and mystical union on the other.

—— .:. ——

Man's spiritual alchemy comprises two dimensions, or two phases, which can be designated by the terms "doctrine" and "method", or "truth" and "way". The first element appears as the divine Word, and the second as the human response; in this sense the truth is a descent, and the way an ascent.

That being said, let us return to our starting point. *Ātmā* became *Māyā* so that *Māyā* might become *Ātmā*;[11] the reason for this is that the divine All-Possibility, which coincides with Infinitude, implies the possibility for God to be known "from without" and starting from an "other than He"; therein lies the whole meaning of the creation of man, and even of creation as such. At the level of Being, the Sovereign Good becomes differentiated, and the resulting qualities become exteriorized; without an Absolute making itself Relativity, there would be no world.

Certainly, the cosmogonic projection brings about distance from God, but this is in the sense of a *felix culpa*; the Bible attests to this: "And God saw that it was good." In Buddhist language: "May all beings be happy"; this is to say that beyond the cycles of existence the last word belongs to Beatitude, which coincides with Being, and thereby with the essence of all that is.

---

[10] "Inasmuch as ye have done it unto one of the least of these my brethren, ye have done it unto Me." The divine Self is subjectively immanent in ourselves and objectively immanent in others; objectively from our point of view, but subjectively from theirs, for they are "I" just as we are.

[11] We paraphrase here in Vedantic terms the famous formula of Saint Irenaeus, which enunciates the reciprocity between God and man and thereby the cosmogonic circuit. For the human microcosm this circuit concludes in Paradise; for the macrocosm—the "universal Man" (*al-Insān al-Kāmil*) of the Sufis—the end result is the *apocatastasis*.

The Play of Masks

When humanity is considered from the standpoint of its values, it is necessary to distinguish *a priori* between man-as-center, who is determined by the intellect and is therefore rooted in the Immutable, and man-as-periphery, who is more or less an accident. This difference is repeated—*mutatis mutandis*—in every man who is conscious of the supernatural, whether he belongs to the first category or the second; without this awareness there is no authentic centrality nor consequently any decisive worth. That is the meaning of the Eckhartian *distinguo* between the "inner man" and the "outer man": the latter is passively identified with his experiences, whereas the former may enjoy or suffer in his temporal humanity while remaining impassible in his immortal kernel, which coincides with his state of union with God. The possibility of such a parallelism lies in man's very nature, and is the essence of the notion of the *avatāra*; in this respect—analogically speaking and with all due proportion—every "pneumatic" is "true man and true God". The underlying divine substance does not abolish the human mask, any more than the mask prevents the divine manifestation.[1]

It has been said that there are saintly men who "laugh with those who laugh and weep with those who weep"; which indirectly expresses the detachment, and directly the good will, of the "pneumatic" or "central" man. He is detached because he does not identify with the accidents; and he is good-willed because, for that very reason, he could be neither egoistic nor petty; but his very superiority poses for him problems of adaptation, for on the one hand he must form part of the human ambience, and on the other he cannot grasp immediately all its absurdity.[2] Man-as-center is necessarily situated in an isolation from which he

[1] The play of Krishna with the *gopīs* refers to the mask; the apparition of his immutable form before Arjuna refers to the divine Substance. This form, reflected in *Māyā*, assumed in its turn innumerable masks, not earthly but celestial.

[2] In *Hamlet*, Shakespeare puts forth the image of a contemplative but dreamy and passional man: in the first respect, the hero remains a stranger to the absurdity of the world; in the second, he himself becomes enmeshed in this incoherence. It should be noted that the work of a playwright of necessity refers to the cosmic phenomenon of the innumerable masks that differentiate the human person; natural masks that are unaware of being masks, precisely, whereas an actor is aware of it and thereby can "realize" the profound meaning of his protean art. The emperor Augustus, who was

cannot but suffer "outwardly": feeling that every man is in a certain way like himself, he sincerely puts himself in their place, but it is far from the case that others put themselves in his. Moreover, the ways of acting of the man-as-center may be "amoral", although not "immoral": they may be contrary to a particular morality, but not to morality as such; that is to say, it is proper to discern between a "justice" that is extrinsic and conditional and another that is intrinsic and unconditional.

On the other hand and in a general way, it is obviously necessary to distinguish between the mask of charity and the mask of malice; the latter is insincere, the former is sincere. In ordinary language, the word "mask" is synonymous with "false appearance", hence with insincerity; this is plausible from the standpoint of ordinary psychology, but it is to lose sight of the fact that there are sacred masks and priestly vestments, which express either what transcends the wearer, or on the contrary express his transcendent substance itself. This, moreover, is how in historical religions an *upāya* serves as the vestment of the "naked truth", namely the primordial, perennial, and universal religion: symbolism transmits the heavenly Message and at the same time conceals the provisionally unassimilable mystery.

There is a difference in function, in principle at least, between the veil and the mask: the mask is positive in the sense that it expresses, affirms, manifests, whereas the veil is negative because it hides and thus renders inaccessible. We could also say that, by the veil one wishes "to appear less than one is" since one wants "to disappear"; by the mask, on the contrary, one wishes to appear to be "more than one is", since one's intention is to express something that one is not, unless the mask serves to manifest the very "heart" of the wearer and to specify thereby a personal value—which actually is transpersonal—and which otherwise would remain invisible. However, there are cases wherein wisdom takes on the appearance of naivety—or even absurdity—whether involuntarily through lack of experience in an inferior environment,[3] or voluntarily in virtue of a vocation of concealing

divinized while still living, is supposed to have said before dying: "Applaud, for have I not played well the comedy of life?" This indicates in its way the distance of the "pneumatic" in relation to the "psychic" and the "hylic".

[3] However: "Whoso can do the greater, can do the lesser"; this is obvious, but it presupposes that the ambience be intelligible to the superior man situated in it, for he may not understand the psychological functioning of a given sin or vice; he comes from "another planet", and moreover bears it within himself.

wisdom, and thereby of ostentatious paradox;[4] this possibility is one that cannot be excluded from the gamut of human attitudes, nor with all the more reason from divine All-Possibility.

We mentioned above the isolation of the man-as-center in the face of the world's absurdity; now the fact that aspects of his behavior can be like that of the man-as-periphery may give the impression of solidarity with the worldly ambience, but this is a misleading appearance, since similar ways of acting can hide dissimilar intentions. Aside from the fact that the superior man may behave "like others" to mask his superiority, precisely—either out of charity or out of an "instinct for self-preservation"—there is this to consider, and it is essential: for the contemplative man, pleasure does not inflate his individuality; on the contrary, it invites to a transpersonal dilation, so that the "sensible consolation" gives rise to an upward opening and not to a downward inflation.[5] Moreover, an analogous grace intervenes for every sincere believer when he approaches pleasure "in the name of God" and thus opens himself to Mercy: he "invites" God and at the same time takes refuge in Him.

The moral norm—given human weakness—may be "counter to nature", extrinsically speaking; however, it is not so intrinsically. "They have no wine", said Mary at the wedding at Cana, with an

---

[4] The names of Diogenes and Omar Khayyam, and perhaps even those of Nasruddin Khoja and Till Eulenspiegel, could be cited here. The court fools pertain in principle to the same rather ambiguous category as do the *heyoka* of the American Indians, not to mention the "fools of God" who can be encountered in various religious environments.

[5] The character of pleasure, in principle equivocal, appears in a particularly flagrant manner in music, which is intoxicating in two opposite directions, self-love and the sense of the Infinite; it can invite to narcissism just as much as to contemplative self-transcending. Meister Eckhart wrote somewhere that every meal has a sacramental import for souls deeply united to God; thus pleasure, to the extent of its effectiveness, excludes the mechanism of a passional lapse, whether the person involved be a hermit or polygamous. "Water takes on the color of its receptacle", said Al-Junayd, which implies that pleasure takes on the nature of the man enjoying it; in other words, the nature of the subject determines the relationship between the subject and the object.

intention that could not be limited to the "flesh", any more than the symbolisms of the Song of Songs or of the *Gītā Govinda*. Ascesis is useful or necessary for man such as he is in fact—for man excluded from the earthly and heavenly Paradises—but the ascetical perspective could not for all that have the prerogatives proper to the whole truth, nor consequently with legitimacy pure and simple. The partisans of a touchy asceticism readily overlook the fact that men are not all alike: no doubt, every amusement is a pleasure, but it does not follow that every pleasure is an amusement, otherwise every marriage would be something frivolous, including the wedding at Cana.

It is not only truth, merit, and sacrifice that lead to God, but also beauty; creation itself testifies to this, then sacred art, including liturgy, the forms of worship. It is not only error, crime, and lust that remove from God, but also ugliness; yet not so when ugliness is accidental—for then it is neutral[6]—but when it is willed and produced, as is the case of that universe of organized and appalling ugliness which is the modern world. Besides, vice is a kind of ugliness, just as virtue is a kind of beauty; "thou art all fair, my love, there is no spot in thee."

Man's deiformity implies moral beauty, be it only—*de facto*—in its capacity as potentiality. The pneumatic is a man who identifies *a priori* with his spiritual substance and thus always remains true to himself; he is not a mask unaware of the one bearing it, as is the case for the man enclosed in accidentality.

Jīvātmā, the "living soul", is the mask-as-individual illusorily and innumerably superimposed on *Ātmā*, or on the one "Self". Now the individual as such identifies itself with contingency, and, as a result, is subject to the principles of limitation and fluctuation; limitation, because no formal perfection can include all other perfections, and fluctuation, because temporal manifestation is subject to phases or to alternations—namely, to activity and passivity—and although this

---

[6] And neutralized by a context of beauty; herein lies, in a certain sense, the meaning of the gargoyles on cathedrals. Likewise, one does not blame a man for being ugly, but one may blame him for the ugliness of his expression.

takes away nothing from perfection as such, it can nonetheless disfigure it. The phase of activity favors man's natural freedom; but the phase of passivity renders man more vulnerable in relation to his ambience and also to his own weaknesses, be they substantial or accidental. In a word, contingency is made of disparities, in time as in space, without this necessarily implying—it must be stressed—intrinsic imperfections.[7] Let us specify that there is not only the temporal fluctuation between the active and passive phases, but also the as it were spatial disequilibrium between man's outward and inward dimensions; the ideal is, on the one hand, the victory of spiritual activity over the passive phase, and on the other, the victory of spiritual inwardness over the outward dimension.

The problem of equilibrium is particularly related to the tugging back and forth between the exteriorizing or manifesting function and the interiorizing or reintegrating function: there are sages whose sole duty is to attract souls towards the "within", and this is the rule; there are others who add to this function that of creating sensible supports, and this is the exception; the most obvious and eminent example of this is the "culture hero" (*Kulturheros*) who inaugurates a civilization or a period of culture.[8] And the following *distinguo* is essential: there is an exteriorization that is profane and amounts to a choice of the "world" as against the spirit; there is another that is spiritual, whose aim is interiorization, the way towards the "kingdom of God"; for every man endowed with the merest of spiritual inclinations, the criterion of the balance between the outward and the inward is the predominance of the internal pole of attraction. The "man of prayer" is capable of measuring what he is able to offer to his ambience, and what he is able to accept from it, without dispersing himself and without being unfaithful to his vocation of inwardness; nothing should be to the detriment of our relationship with immanent Heaven. Only those who give themselves to God can know what they have the right, or duty, to give to the world and to receive from it.

---

[7] This is what explains the states of "aridity" or "dryness" from which mystics may suffer; in these states they are particularly exposed to temptations or to inner trials.

[8] By painting the first icon of the Blessed Virgin, Saint Luke introduced painting into Christianity and created the entire artistic dimension of this religion, which has been maintained in the Eastern Church. In an analogous manner, Jalal ad-Din Rumi introduced music and dance into Sufism, not through invention, of course, but through inspiration.

Aside from limitation, fluctuation, and disequilibrium, there is impermanence, which is temporal limitation; in one and the same life, childhood, youth, maturity pass, as does life itself.[9] Normally, youth and maturity constitute the manifestation of the prototype or the "idea", for childhood and old-age have something privative in them: the child is "not yet", and the old man is "no longer". Be that as it may, the summit of individual manifestation is not always situated in youth or in maturity: some individuals manifest their best possibility in childhood, after which they harden or become heavyset; others manifest it only in old age. Of course, a peak manifestation at maturity need not preclude the same from occurring in old age: an *avatāra*, who is of necessity a perfect man in every respect, will necessarily manifest the perfection of each age; this is also possible for men of a less lofty category, and even for individuals who are modestly endowed but nonetheless marked by a heavenly favor.

"The righteous man sins seven times a day": the point of this contradiction in terms is to help us understand that in this lower world perfection cannot be absolute, except in the sense of the "relatively absolute"; without this reservation, one would be able to do without the notion of perfection. According to Muslim esoterism, "There is no sin comparable with that of existence"; thus the Sufi asks forgiveness of God morning and night, possibly without being aware of any wrongdoing;[10] he accuses himself because he exists. "Why callest thou me good?" said Christ; "there is none good but one, that is, God"; which obviously could not mean that there is the least blemish in deified man.

---

[9] "All that appears deserves to disappear" (*Denn alles, was entsteht, ist wert, dass es zugrunde geht*), said Goethe in his *Faust*, wherein he confuses moreover God's destructive function with the corrosive function of the devil; the saying nonetheless expresses a certain "logic" inherent in creaturely *Māyā*.

[10] If David considered that "mine iniquities . . . are more than the hairs of mine head", it is because, as a Semitic fideist and moralist—not a "philosopher" as the Aryan Greeks and Hindus—he "subjectivizes" his objective awareness of the dissonances of relativity.

If, on the one hand, man is subject to limitations, dimensions, phases—owing in large measure to his connection with matter—on the other hand, he can be either fundamentally good or fundamentally bad, depending on his individual substance which, for its part, pertains to the play of All-Possibility; it is the possibilities that "want" to be what they are, it is not God who imposes it upon them. And this is unrelated to the general modes of contingency such as space and time; the direct cause of personal character resides not in matter, nor in other external factors, but in the spirit, in the individual sense of this term. The righteous manifest qualities, the iniquitous on the contrary manifest privations; but both alike are subject to the vicissitudes of existence.

The combination of all the fundamental characters and the modes of earthly contingency gives rise to an indefinite diversity of types and destinies;[11] thus the relativists will conclude that nothing is good or evil in itself, there are only degrees of "more" and "less", which is flagrant nonsense. It is to overlook a distinction—apparently absurd yet metaphysically essential—which we have mentioned above, namely the distinction between the "pure absolute" and the "relatively absolute"; the first is the good as such, and the second, the good through participation, or the good "projected into the stuff of evil", if one may so express it.[12]

We have said above that the limitations, dimensions, and phases that govern man may result from his connection with matter; in fact, they govern only the physical and the psychic and not intelligence as such; *corpus* and *anima* and not *spiritus*. The body and the soul are two masks superimposed on the spirit, which in its substance remains unlimited and immutable; and this takes us back to the Eckhartian concept of the "inner man".

Perhaps we should add here a consideration that, although not pertaining directly to our subject, is nonetheless connected with it.

[11] "Whoso willeth, cannot; whoso can, willeth not; whoso knoweth, doeth not; whoso doeth, knoweth not; and thus it goeth ill with the world" (*Chi vuo, non puo; chi puo, non vuo; chi sa, non fa; chi fa, non sa; e così il mondo mal va*). This Italian saying, with its proverbial quality, in its way sums up well the misery of the "human comedy", and *ipso facto* that of earthly contingency.

[12] The notion of the "relatively absolute" could not imply that there is an "absolutely relative", for this expression—aside from its intrinsic absurdity—is practically synonymous with "nothingness".

According to a Hindu expression, "The Lord is the only transmigrant", which means He goes from birth to birth crossing the chain of the worlds. This is true in the sense of *līlā*, the "divine play", but not if one concludes that individuals are not real at their own level and that they are not responsible for their actions.[13]

Our profound identity is our relationship with God; our mask is the form that we must assume in the world of forms, of space, of time. Our ambience, as well as our personality, necessarily pertain to the particular, not to the Universal; to possible being, not to necessary Being; to the relative good, not to the Sovereign Good. Thus, there is no need to be disturbed because one lives in a given ambience and not in another; furthermore, there is no need to be disturbed because one is a specific individual rather than some other. Being a person—on pain of nonexistence—one must needs be a particular person; that is, "such and such a person" and not the "person as such"; the latter is situated only in the world of the divine Ideas, whereas the former is its reflection within contingency.

What matters is to maintain, starting from possible being, the contact with necessary Being; with the Sovereign Good that is the essence of our relative values, and whose merciful nature includes the desire to save us from ourselves; to deliver us by having us participate in its mystery both living and immutable.

[13] It should not be overlooked that it is as a consequence of their actions that individuals transmigrate, and that the immanent transmigration of the Lord pertains to the onto-cosmological dimension and not to that of concordant actions and reactions. See the chapter "Eschatologie universelle" in our book *Sur les traces de la Religion pérenne*.

Ex Nihilo, In Deo

In the expression *creatio ex nihilo*, the word *nihil* determines the meaning of the word *ex*: thus *ex* does not presuppose a substance or a container, as is normally the case, it simply indicates the possibility in principle—which possibility is denied precisely by the word *nihil* in regard to creation—rather as the word "with" indicates a possible object even in the expression "with nothing", which in fact means "without object". Hence there is no point in blaming the theological formula in question for suggesting an extra-divine substance and thereby a fundamental dualism;[1] that would amount to playing with words and taking too seriously the minor pitfalls of language.

Obviously, creation "derives"—that is the meaning of the word *ex*—from an origin; not from a cosmic, hence "created" substance, but from a reality pertaining to the Creator, and in this sense—and in this sense only—it can be said that creation is situated in God. It is situated in Him from the perspective of ontological immanence: each thing in fact "contains"—on pain of being non-existent—Being, on the one hand, and a given Archetype or "Idea", on the other; the divine "content" is *ipso facto* also the "container", and even is so *a priori*, since God is Reality as such. But things are "outside God"—all sacred Scriptures attest to this—from the perspective of contingency, hence as regards the concrete phenomena of the world; the Sovereign Good could not be the content of that privative existence—or of that abyss of contingency—that is evil. The ontological and hence "neutral" structure of evil is "in God", but not so evil itself; in other words, privative and subversive possibilities are *in Deo* only inasmuch as they testify to Being and therefore to All-Possibility, but not by their negative contents, which paradoxically signify non-existence or the impossible, hence the absurd.

It may be objected that in situating a dimension of the world outside God we postulate an irreducible dualism; this is in fact what we are doing, but it is on the plane of universal Relativity—the cosmic *Māyā*[2]—which by definition coincides with duality. The absurdity

---

[1] God fashioned Adam "of earth"; but earth was created *ex nihilo*, and with it Adam.

[2] Not metacosmic or divine *Māyā*, which is the same as pure Being, the personal God, the Creator.

of "two realities" is precisely the mystery of Relativity; it is the possibility of an "other than God"; to say that there are things which are "outside God", means that they are "in *Māyā*". To eliminate this "outside God"—by maintaining that "everything is in God" in every respect—is to eliminate *Māyā*, mystery of Infinitude and of "divine paradox".

There are those who, intending to solve the problem of evil, have maintained that for God evil does not exist, and consequently that for Him everything is a good, which is inadmissible and ill-sounding. What ought to be said is that God sees the privative manifestations only in connection with the positive manifestations that compensate for them; thus, evil is a provisional factor in view of a greater good, of a "victory of the Truth"; *vincit omnia Veritas.*

At the supreme degree of Reality—*Ātmā* or *Brahman*—*Māyā* neither "is" nor "exists"; consequently, the question of dualities, of oppositions, of good and evil, could not arise. At the degree of metacosmic *Māyā*, the complementary oppositions assert themselves—God is at once Rigor and Gentleness, Justice and Mercy, Power and Beauty—but contingency, and with it evil, are absent; it is only at the degree of cosmic *Māyā*—this shifting fabric of circumstances and antinomies—that the "existential vices" can be produced, at one and the same time "in God" and "outside God": "in God", in the sense that every possibility necessarily pertains to All-Possibility, and "outside God" because the Sovereign Good can only contain the archetypal possibilities, which by definition are positive since they describe the potentialities of pure Being.

— .:. —

In what follows, our intention is not needlessly to recall an axiom of which no metaphysician is unaware; our intention is simply to draw attention to two different but complementary delimitations of the "space" *Ātmā-Māyā*, which renders certain repetitions unavoidable.

Hence, one knows that there are two "ontological regions", the Absolute and the Relative; the first consists of Beyond-Being, and the second, of both Being and Existence, of the Creator and Creation. But there is also another possible distribution of the same realities; in other words, we may envisage two other "regions", namely the Principial and the Manifested; the first category comprises Beyond-Being and Being—this is the "divine Order"—and the second, Existence, the Universe, the world. This means that Being does not coincide with the "pure Absolute"; it pertains to the divine Order inasmuch as it is a direct reflection of the Absolute in the Relative, and consequently it is what may be termed paradoxically the "relatively absolute". If the personal God were the Absolute as such, He could not be an interlocutor for man.

The relationship *Ātmā-Māyā* is indirectly affirmed—at the extremity of the cosmogonic trajectory—by two new "regions", the heavenly and the earthly; we say "indirectly" because the celestial world is *Ātmā* only by analogy, in the sense that it is the reflection of the Principle within Manifestation, thus conferring upon it, in relation to the world of imperfection and impermanence, a quasi-divine function. Hence, the mythologies readily present the "heavens" as the extreme limit of the divine Order, and not as an infra-divine category; the angels and the archangels of the Semitic cosmologies thus appear as "gods"—the *devas*—who, starting from Perfection, govern the imperfect world.

Only the celestial or angelic Center can escape the fissures and vicissitudes of the cosmic periphery—of the inferior *Māyā* or of the *Samsāra*—without thereby being able to escape the limitations proper to Relativity. This *distinguo* is essential: "limitation" is not synonymous with "imperfection"; the sphere is limited in relation to space, but it is in no way imperfect, quite the contrary since it is the most perfect form possible. In saying that "God alone is good", Christ meant to specify, not that the angels and the blessed are deprived of goodness, but that only the principial Order—hence the non-manifested—is situated beyond even the accidental possibility of imperfection.

"Our Father who art in heaven", said Christ, thereby indicating the two poles of the divine Order, namely the God-Person and the celestial world. "Hallowed be Thy Name", and "Thy Kingdom come": the first of these sayings evokes the ascent of *Māyā* towards *Ātmā*, of man towards God; and the second, the descent of *Ātmā* towards *Māyā*, of God towards man; this is also expressed—with a different accentuation—by the patristic formula: "God became man that man might become God." The Essence limited itself by form so that the form might be liberated by the Essence: the reason for being of the finite is, not only the differentiated and innumerable manifestation of

33

the Infinite, but also that perfection, or that bliss, which is the return to it.

We have said that each ontological degree presents an aspect of either center or periphery according to whether its context is inferior or superior. But there is more: each degree possesses in itself these two aspects, starting with the "dimensions" of absoluteness and infinitude in Beyond-Being; analogously, Being comprises intrinsic and extrinsic qualities, it is "holy" or "wise" in its essence and "just" or "merciful" towards creation. In Heaven, it is possible to distinguish between the supreme Angel—or the Archangels combined—and the other angels, to which are joined the blessed; beneath Heaven, in the "round of births and deaths", the motionless mover—as Aristotle would say—is none other than man who, being "made in the image of God", is open to the Absolute and to Deliverance. Man *ipso facto* represents the Immutable and the Limitless, to the extent that the extreme limit of universal Manifestation makes this possible; he represents them potentially, indirectly, and passively in the case of ordinary men, but effectively, directly, and actively in the case of deified man, who then is central not only—as is every man—with regard to the animal world, but also—in a particular and additional manner—with regard to the multitude of ordinary men. The "believers" are like the *gopīs* dancing around Krishna and uniting themselves to him; whereas he—the "motionless mover"—plays the saving flute.

To say that deified man plays the part of the motionless mover in relation to a human collectivity, means implicitly that Revelation, Tradition, the divine Symbol, or the sacred in general represent this mover. As an example of the Symbol—or of symbolism—we shall mention the circumambulation of the Kaaba,[3] primordial sanctuary; in this rite, the movement is circular like the revolution of the planets. Another example is the Sun Dance around a tree representing the axis Heaven-Earth; there the movement is alternatively centripetal and

---

[3] This rite is much more ancient than Islam, since it goes back to Abraham; originally, the participants were naked—like the Indians and in part like the *gopīs*—which Islam modified by instituting the semi-nudity of the pilgrims.

centrifugal like the phases of respiration, which takes us back to the dance of the *gopīs* with its two modes, namely circumambulation and union. The universal symbol of the wheel combines both types of participation, which refer, finally, to the two fundamental relationships between *Ātmā* and *Māyā*, the analogical and the unitive: manifestation of diversifying Potentiality and reintegration into the original Synthesis.

In the Face of Contingency

What makes us happy are the phenomena of beauty and goodness and all the other goods that existence borrows from pure Being; what adds shadows to them is contingency, to which they pertain by force of circumstance since, precisely, they exist. Contingency not only causes all kinds of limitations, and above all imperfection and impermanence, but it also sets positive phenomena in opposition to negative phenomena, and necessarily so, since All-Possibility is infinite and consequently cannot exclude privative possibilities; these cannot but seem absurd, yet all told that is their reason for being.

We are situated in contingency, but we live by the reflections of the Absolute, otherwise we could not exist. We live in and by those agents of contingency that are space, time, form, number, matter, individuality; within this framework, each thing that we love is irreplaceable insofar as it is a celestial message, a ray of the Absolute, but at the same time each thing could be different, including our personality; and this plunges us into a climate of relativity, ambiguity, indefiniteness, and inflicts upon us temptations of incertitude and ingratitude.[1] Wisdom is not only to see the archetype through the form or the heavenly in the earthly, it is also to be resigned to contingency; we have no choice but to be someone and to be someplace, even if we are aware of the possibility of being someone else and of being somewhere else, that is, of experiencing a given element of happiness in another form.

There are here two spiritual attitudes or two fundamental virtues to realize, namely resignation to contingency and assimilation of the celestial message. Assimilation first by gratitude and then by interiorization; for everything lies in discovering that ontologically we bear within ourselves that which we love and which in the final analysis constitutes our reason for being. The indetermination—or the fluc-

---

[1] Hamlet's drama is that of an *a priori* superior man who immerses—and encloses—himself in contingency, thereby losing contact with the Absolute; the atmosphere of his "complex" of duty and vengeance is tragically incompatible with that of his love for the angelic Ophelia, a love which would have saved him had he understood that love has precedence over hatred and moreover is not opposed to duty. It will be recalled that according to Aristotle, the goal of tragedy is a *katharsis*, a "purification" through the striking spectacle of miseries due to human absurdity.

tuation—of contingency can neither trouble nor overcome us if we realize within ourselves the meaning of the celestial contents.

Just as there is a discernment of principial realities, which is incumbent upon us because we have an intelligence, so too there is a discernment of formal realities—aesthetic as well as moral—which is incumbent upon us because we have a soul. This is to say that metaphysical comprehension must be accompanied by a sense of beauty at every level; conversely, there is no interiorization of the beautiful without a parallel metaphysical knowledge. "Beauty is the splendor of the true": which implies that truth, hence reality, is the essence of beauty.

The ontological coincidence between the true and the beautiful brings up the question of knowing "why" something is deemed beautiful; according to the subjectivists, it is because it pleases us—which is absurd—whereas in reality it pleases an intelligent and normal man because it is beautiful, which however does not answer the question of knowing what beauty consists of concretely. Moreover, one has to know what constitutes not only beauty as such, but also a particular beauty; that is to say, every harmonious and positively expressive thing is beautiful at once in a general respect and in a particular respect. In a general way, every beautiful thing communicates to us beauty as such, namely the Harmony—or Beatitude—of the Sovereign Good; at the same time and in a particular way, it transmits this Harmony according to a particular aspect or a particular order of contingency, and that is necessarily so since the effect cannot possess the essentiality or the totality of the cause. The human body, for example, is beautiful—in its perfect and normative form—not only because it expresses the dimension *Ānanda* proper to *Ātmā*, but also, and additionally, because it expresses it either in masculine mode or in feminine mode[2] or according to a particular racial language; or again, quite obviously, according to a particular individual possibility; or, as regards its specific form: it expresses or manifests the adaptation of

---

[2] Woman manifests beauty as such, so much so that there is no beauty superior to hers, when contingency has not separated her from her prototype; thus, one may discern in beauty as such features of femininity, of passive perfection, of virginal purity, of maternal generosity; of goodness and love.

an integral subjectivity—integral, hence rooted in the consciousness of the Absolute—to a given contingent ambience, namely the earthly world with its categories, its demands, its possibilities; this adaptation is perfect, which is to say that it is in conformity with the nature of Being, and this conformity constitutes an additional element of beauty. Aside from human beauty, there are of course also animal, vegetable, mineral beauties; and from quite another standpoint, there are visual, auditive, mental, and psychic beauties, and others still.

Beauty has something peace-giving and dilating in it, something consoling and liberating, because it communicates a substance of truth, of evidence, and of certitude, and does so in a concrete and existential mode; thus, it is like a mirror of our transpersonal and eternally blissful essence. This being said, it is important not to lose sight of the fact that in the juxtaposition between contingency and the celestial contents projected into it and of which it is the vehicle, it is not solely a question of beauty properly so called—whether of the aesthetic or the moral order—it is also a question of every other factor, large or small, that can legitimately contribute to our happiness; these contents always refer, in indefinitely diverse ways, to celestial Harmony, into which contingency could not bring any privation, any dissonance, any absurdity; in principle we have the right to this Harmony because it is the norm and because it resides in our very substance. And that is why it could be repeated again and again that man's vocation and duty is to become what he is, precisely by freeing himself, inwardly, from the encroaching shadows of this contingent, imperfect, and transitory world.

When one speaks of earthly contingency, it is impossible not to mention matter, which in a certain respect is the vehicle *par excellence* of this contingency: like *Māyā*, matter is spiritually transparent and it can concretely be the vehicle of the celestial messages, but it can also be the door towards that which is below and it has even subjugated humanity by impurity, sickness, old age, and death, so much so that its domain will always be an exile for man. Nonetheless, it must be emphasized, the flowers of Paradise are always within reach; exile is but a dream, because contingency is but a veil.

This mention of matter furnishes us the opportunity to make the following remark concerning materialism: nothing is more contradictory than to deny the spirit, or even simply the psychic element, in favor of matter alone, for it is the spirit that denies, whereas matter remains inert and unconscious. The fact that matter can be conceptualized proves precisely that materialism contradicts itself at its starting point, rather as with Pyrrhonism, for which it is true that there is no truth, or with relativism, for which all is relative except this affirmation. Be that as it may, the subjective could not arise from the objective, and to believe otherwise is to understand nothing of subjectivity; the reverse error also exists, with certain people who conclude from the *Vedānta* that the world is a production of our mind, when in fact our mind is capable neither of creating nor of preventing the existence of any object. True, the world is a dream, but this dream is not ours since we are its contents; the absolute Subject escapes us as much as does the absolute Object, hence as much as does their supreme indistinction.

— ⋅⋮⋅ —

Contingency implies essentially two principles, that of relativity and that of absoluteness; the latter corresponds geometrically to radii, and the former to concentric circles, given that one refers to the center and the other to the periphery.[3] The principle of relativity requires that things appear other than what they are in fact; within this deceptive appearance, and by compensation, the principle of absoluteness requires that things be symbolically adequate, that is, in conformity with their reality. But when the principle of absoluteness predominates, the principle of relativity insinuates itself in the sense that adequate realities are in some fashion limited and consequently do not coincide at every point with their metacosmic prototypes.

For example, the principle of relativity requires that the sun and the stellar vault seem to turn around the earth, but this deceptive appearance could not prevent an intervention of the principle of absoluteness, namely that the sun have precedence over all the other luminaries by its size, its luminosity, its heat, and moreover that the appearance of the solar and stellar movements symbolize adequately the cosmic cycles and the activity of the heavenly powers in relation to the passivity of the material and psychic world.[4] And likewise, but conversely: the principle of absoluteness requires that the sun, in conformity with objective reality, be the center of the planets' revolution;

[3] It is significant that Einstein, the promoter of relativism, found "distasteful" the idea that the universe possesses a center.

[4] It is in virtue of this analogy between an optical illusion and cosmological realities that Ptolemean astronomy comprises an aspect of "exact science".

all the same, the principle of relativity must occur, and it does so by showing, not that the solar orb is not the center of its system, but that it is merely a speck of dust amongst other centers and other systems. The image of the sun as unique center is thus an optical illusion in its turn; God alone is "the Center" without any possible reservations.

If one looks at the universe exclusively with the eyes of relativity, one will see only relative things and the universe will be reduced in the final analysis to an inextricable absurdity. If, however, one sees it with the eyes of absoluteness—of the participation of things in the Absolute—one will essentially see manifestations of the Supreme Principle and, correlatively, images making explicit the relationships between *Ātmā* and *Māyā*.

For the relativists, there is only *Māyā*; but this is contradictory since *Māyā* exists only through its contents, which prolong *Ātmā*; this is to say that *Ātmā* is conceivable without *Māyā*, whereas *Māyā* is intelligible only through the notion of *Ātmā*. Relativity is a projection of the Absolute, or it is nothing; if it is something, that is because the Absolute by definition is also the Infinite and, *ipso facto*, universal radiation as well. That is why the principle of absoluteness implies a principle of infinitude by virtue of which it is impossible to measure the existential categories in an exhaustive fashion.

No doubt the plane of contingency comprises a principle of finitude which entails that everything be limited, and which the skeptics readily lay claim to. But this principle—obviously limited—could not prevent the positive contents of contingency from being derived from the principle of infinitude, owing to the fact that they manifest the essences and therefore All-Possibility.

There is in contingency an element of indefiniteness and unintelligibility, one might say of "irrationality"; scientists want to oblige this element to be logical or to yield secrets that, precisely, it does not possess, or does not possess in an assimilable form. To wish to force things is to expose oneself to becoming the plaything of a "genius of absurdity" inherent in cosmic *Māyā*—the power of illusion, and also of seduction, whose absence in the economy of universal Possibility is metaphysically inconceivable, and one of whose signs is the serpent in the terrestrial Paradise.[5]

---

[5] The tempter pushed man into the descending spiroidal path, that of the indefinite, of the accidental, of contingency without end; one must beware, though, of understanding this in an exclusively moral sense.

41

One may object that contingency can be equated with relativity and thus encompasses, at its summit, the creative Principle—the "personal God"—and with all the more reason the celestial world; to this we reply that the notion of contingency coincides with that of relativity only in the infra-celestial order, which symbolically we may qualify as "terrestrial", and not in the celestial and divine orders, which from the standpoint of contingency—hence of the "earth"—are related to the Absolute,[6] either indirectly or directly.[7] This does not mean that in Heaven there is no possibility that one could term contingent—otherwise there would be no freedom for the blessed—but this contingency is intrinsically determined, and in a sense stabilized and regulated, by the omnipresence of Grace and by the permanence of the beatific vision; we are here, not beyond *Māyā*, of course, but beyond "Transmigration", beyond *Samsāra*.

However that may be, there is certainly a need to distinguish between contingency and relativity. Contingency is always relative, but relativity is not always contingent; one will term relative that which is either "more" or "less" in relation to another reality;[8] that is contingent which may or may not be, hence which is merely possible. In contingency, as in relativity, there are degrees: man as such comprises eminently more ontological necessity than a particular man, and yet he is contingent in relation to the Creator, who in a certain sense is the Absolute "projected" into relativity, or relativity "prefigured" in the Absolute; therein lies the whole mystery of the initial contact between *Ātmā* and *Māyā*.

[6] This leads us back to the idea—paradoxical, but in no way absurd—of the "relatively absolute", which has been discussed more than once in our books.

[7] This is to say that Being and Beyond-Being (*Īshvara* and *Paramātmā*) "constitute" Divinity—at least from the standpoint of Being, for Beyond-Being suffices unto itself—whereas the celestial order "participates" in Divinity in the most direct fashion possible.

[8] Thus, the Creator—Being—is "more" than creation and creatures, but "less" than the pure Absolute—Beyond-Being—which has no interlocutor.

In geometric symbolism, the radii indicate the celestial archetypes or the "ideas"; and the concentric circles, the orders of contingency. This *distinguo* between the celestial content and contingency imposes upon man—who is related to both—a fundamental and decisive choice: to maintain contact with the celestial or the universal by directing himself towards God, or on the contrary to lose this contact and become immersed in the contingent and finally rise up against God; hence ultimately against himself, since beneath the veil of contingency man is attached ontologically to That which is.

The reason for being of the radiation—necessarily centrifugal—of the celestial possibilities is the manifestation of the Sovereign Good; the meaning of evil being this manifestation when it operates by means of contrast; as Meister Eckhart said: "The more he blasphemeth, the more he praiseth God." Direct and analogous manifestation on the one hand, and indirect and contrastive manifestation on the other—both modes being realized in keeping with the infinitude of the divine Possible.

A word concerning metaphysical certitude, or the infallibility of pure intellection, is perhaps called for here. "I think, therefore I am", said Descartes; aside from the fact that our existence is not proven by thought alone, he should have added: "I am, therefore Being is"; or he could have said in the first place: "I think because I am." In any event, the foundation of metaphysical certitude is the coincidence between truth and our being; a coincidence that no ratiocination could invalidate. Contingent things are proven by factors situated within their order of contingency, whereas things deriving from the Absolute become clear by their participation in the Absolute, hence by a "superabundance of light"—according to Saint Thomas—which amounts to saying that they are proven by themselves. In other words, universal truths draw their evidence not from our contingent thought, but from our transpersonal being, which constitutes the substance of our spirit and guarantees the adequacy of intellection.

Contingency on the one hand and presence of the Absolute on the other; these are the two poles of our existence. The divine presence coincides with our consciousness—or with our intellectual and moral evocation—of the Absolute-Infinite, which by definition is the Sovereign Good since all possible goods derive from it and testify to it. This presence-consciousness, or this evocation, is set into space and time: spatial, it excludes the world, which extends indefinitely around us;[9] temporal, it repeats itself and thereby reduces duration, which corrodes us, to the Eternal Present—complement of the Infinite Center—which liberates us.

In principle, this consciousness of God is within every man's reach, precisely because he is man; in fact, it has its exigencies: its formal, ritual, and traditional conditions, because man has radically turned away from his human vocation by plunging into the world of contingency and by identifying himself with it, whence the profane ego with its tyranny and its vices. The salutary—but excessive—reaction to this situation is an asceticism that seems to want to destroy the ego as such, counter to the nature of things or to the intention of the Creator; in reality, what is called for is an equilibrium between our consciousness of the Absolute and the divine Manifestation—made of beauty and goodness—which surrounds us everywhere, and which bids us to the "Kingdom of God which is within you".

—— .:. ——

Being included within the terrestrial *Māyā*, we must maintain the balance between temporal disturbances and eternal values; but we must just as much maintain the balance between the beauties of this world and those of the other: between the terrestrial projections and the celestial archetypes. Or between analogy or resemblance, and abstraction or incomparability—analogy referring to immanence, and abstraction to transcendence.

The sense of beauty actualized by the visual or auditive perception of the beautiful, or by the corporeal manifestation, whether static or dynamic, of beauty, amounts to a "remembrance of God" if it is balanced by the "remembrance of God" properly so called, which on the contrary requires the extinction of the perceptible. The sensible perception of the beautiful must be answered by the withdrawal

[9] The discriminative and contemplative abstraction of the world could not exclude our natural contacts with our ambience, which is not merely Eve, but also Mary. There is parallelism, not incompatibility, between the "remembrance of God" and contingent life.

towards the suprasensible source of beauty; the perception of sensible theophany requires unitive interiorization.

For some, only the forgetting of the beautiful—of the "flesh" according to them—brings us closer to God, which is obviously a valid point of view in a certain operative respect; according to others—and this perspective is more profound—sensible beauty also brings us closer to God, and even *a priori*, on the double condition of a contemplativity that has the presentiment of the archetypes through sensible manifestations, and of an interiorizing spiritual activity that eliminates the sensations in view of the intellective and unitive perception of the Essence.

Delineations of Original Sin

The idea of original sin situates the cause of the human fall in an action; consequently, this fall consists in committing evil actions, or sins, precisely. The disadvantage of this idea—which nonetheless is providential and efficacious—is that a man who commits no manifest transgression may believe himself to be perfect, as if it sufficed to do no evil to deserve Heaven; Christian doctrine guards against this temptation by stressing that every man is a sinner; to doubt this is to add two more sins, those of presumption and heresy. In such an atmosphere, one almost feels obligated, if not to sin, at least to see sins everywhere; it is true that there is a definite number of mortal sins, but the venial sins are innumerable, and they become serious when they are habitual, for then they are vices.

Be that as it may, a reflexive *mea culpa* that has nothing concrete in view, is not a panacea and hardly makes us better; but what is altogether different is to be conscious of the presence in our soul of a tendency to "outwardness" and "horizontality", which constitutes, if not original sin properly so called, at least the hereditary vice that is derived therefrom.

In connection with the idea of sin-as-act, let us note in passing that there are behaviors which are sins objectively without being so subjectively, and that there are others which are sins subjectively without being so objectively: a given saint neglects a religious duty because he is in ecstasy, a given hypocrite accomplishes it because he wishes to be admired. This is said in order to recall that it is the intention of an act which determines its worth; however, it is not enough for the intention to be subjectively good, it must also be so objectively.

But let us return to our subject: to affirm that every man is a "sinner" does not amount to saying that no man is capable of abstaining from evil actions, but it certainly means that every man—with the rarest exceptions—succumbs to the temptations of "outwardness" and "horizontality"; where there is no temptation of excess in the direction of either the outward or the horizontal, there is no longer either concupiscence or impiety.[1] Assuredly, every man has the right

---

[1] Which evokes the case of the "pneumatics" and above all the mystery of the "Immaculate Conception".

to a certain solidarity with his ambience, as is proven by our faculties of sensation and action, but this right is limited by our complementary duty of inwardness, without which we would not be men, precisely; this means that the pole of attraction which is the "kingdom of God within you" must finally prevail over the seductive magic of the world.[2] This is what the supreme Commandment enunciates, which, while teaching us what we must do, also teaches us what we are.

The concept of the sin of omission[3] allows us to grasp more firmly the problem of hereditary sin, that sin which exists in us before our actions. If the requirement of the supreme Commandment is to "love God with all thy heart, and with all thy soul, and with all thy strength, and with all thy mind", it follows that the contrary attitude is the supreme sin, in varying degrees since one has to distinguish between hatred of God and simple indifference; nevertheless, God says in the Apocalypse: "So then because thou art lukewarm . . . I will spue thee out of my mouth." If we wish to give the word "sin" its broadest or deepest meaning, we would say that it expresses above all an attitude of the heart; hence a "being" and not a simple "doing" or "not doing"; in this case, the Biblical myth symbolizes a "substance" and not a simple "accident".

Thus it is that original "sin", for the Hindus, is "nescience" (*avidyā*): ignorance that "*Brahman* is real, the world is illusory", and that "the soul is not other than *Brahman*"; all actions or attitudes contrary to intrinsic and vocational Law (*Dharma*) result from this blindness of heart.

[2] According to Shankara, the one "liberated in this life" (*jīvan-mukta*) is not he who stands apart from all that is human, it is he who, when he "laughs with those who laugh and weeps with those who weep", remains the supernaturally unaffected witness of the "cosmic play" (*līlā*).

[3] According to the Apostle James, he who knows to do good and does not do it, commits a sin; this is the very definition of sin by omission, but at the same time it goes beyond the framework of a formalistic and exoteric morality.

"Horizontality" and "outwardness", we said above. To be "horizontal" is to love only terrestrial life, to the detriment of the ascending and celestial path; to be "exteriorized", is to love only outer things, to the detriment of moral and spiritual values. Or again: horizontality is to sin against transcendence, thus it is to forget God and consequently the meaning of life; and outwardness is to sin against immanence, thus it is to forget our immortal soul and consequently its vocation. In assuming that the original sin would have been an action—whatever the form given to it by a particular mythology—we will say, on the one hand, that this action had as its effect the two kinds of lapses just mentioned, and on the other hand, that these lapses predispose to the indefinite repetition of the original transgression; every sinful action repeats the drama of the forbidden fruit. Primordial perfection was made of "verticality" and "inwardness", as is attested by those two distinctive characteristics of man that are vertical posture and language, the latter coinciding with reason.

Transcendence is objective inasmuch as it concerns the divine Order in itself, immanence is subjective inasmuch as it refers to the divine Presence in us; nonetheless there is also a subjective transcendence, that which within us separates the divine Self from the human "I", and an objective immanence, namely the divine Presence in the world surrounding us. To be really conscious of "God-as-Object" is also to be conscious of His immanence, and to be conscious of "God-as-Subject", is also to be conscious of His transcendence.

Inwardness and verticality, outwardness and horizontality:[4] these are the dimensions that make up man in all his greatness and all his littleness. To speak of transcendence is to speak both of metaphysical Truth and saving Divinity; and to speak of immanence is to speak of transpersonal Intellect and divine Selfhood. Verticality in the face of "our Father who art in heaven" and inwardness in virtue of the "kingdom of God which is within you"; whence a certitude and a serenity that no stratagem of the powers of darkness can take away from us.

---

[4] In accordance with the principle of the double meaning of symbols, inwardness and verticality are not solely positive, any more than outwardness and horizontality are solely negative. Inwardness means not only depth but also subjectivism, egoism, hardness of self; verticality means not only ascension but also the Fall. Similarly, but inversely, outwardness means not only superficiality and dispersion, but also movement towards a center that liberates; and horizontality means not only baseness, but also stability.

Eve and Adam succumbed to the temptation to wish to be more than they could be; the serpent represents the possibility of this temptation. The builders of the Tower of Babel, as well as the Titans, Prometheus, and Icarus, wished to put themselves inappropriately in God's place; they too suffered the humiliating chastisement of a fall. According to the Bible, the forbidden tree was that of the discernment between "good" and "evil"; now this discernment, or this difference, pertains to the very nature of Being, consequently, its source could not be in the creature; to claim it for oneself is to wish to be equal to the Creator, and that is the very essence of sin; of all sin. Indeed, the sinner decides what is good, counter to the objective nature of things; he willingly deludes himself about things and about himself, whence the Fall, which is nothing other than the reaction of reality.

The great ambiguity of the human phenomenon resides in the fact that man is divine without being God: Koranically speaking, man gives all creatures their names, and that is why the angels must prostrate before him; except for the supreme Angel,[5] which indicates that man's divinity, and consequently his authority and autonomy, are relative, although "relatively absolute". Thus it is that the fall of man as such could not be total, as is proven *a priori* by the nature and destiny of the patriarch Enoch, father of all "pneumatics", one might say.

For exoterist ideology, esoterism—"gnosis"—can only originate from darkness since it seems to claim the prerogative of the forbidden tree, the spontaneous and autonomous discernment between "good and evil"; but this is to overlook the essential, namely that *aliquid est in anima quod est increatum et increabile . . . et hoc est Intellectus.*[6] The Fall was, precisely, the rupture between reason and Intellect, the ego and the Self; one could speculate forever on the modes and degrees of this rupture, which on the one hand involves the human species and on the other hand could not be absolute.

---

[5] Or the Archangels, which amounts to the same thing; it is the divine Spirit, which is mirrored directly at the center or the summit of universal Manifestation.

[6] Meister Eckhart: "There is something in the soul which is uncreated and uncreatable . . . and this is the Intellect."

On Intention

The primacy of intention stems from the fact that one and the same action—we are not saying every action—may be good or bad according to the intention, whereas the inverse is not true: an intention is not good or bad according to the action.[1] It is not actions that matter primarily, but rather intentions, as common sense as well as traditional wisdom tell us; all well and good, however it goes without saying that this could not mean, as some people imagine, that every imperfect or even bad action can be excused by supposing that the intention was good or even by arguing that every intention is basically good merely because it is subjective and that, according to some people, subjectivity is always right.

To excuse, if only partially, a blameworthy action or production by arguing that the intention was good, makes sense only in the following cases. First: when the negative result is contrary to what the agent intended; such is the case of a child who starts a fire by lighting a candle. Second: when there are serious reasons for supposing that the badness—or imperfection—of the action or product is due only to an accidental lack of skill; such is the case of an ailing person who is not up to his task. Third: when there are valid reasons for supposing that the intention of a person well-known to be imperfect or bad was good in the case under consideration; to be aware of it is to demonstrate commendable objectivity. Fourth: when the agent is substantially—not accidentally—incapable of executing his project in a satisfactory manner; such is the case of a child who tries to paint a picture, or of a crude or uncultivated man who tries to please with a gift in bad taste, but nonetheless honorable; in this case the intention as such is excused and not the deficiency marring its expression; in the case of the child, even the deficiency is excused, if it is merely a question of age. Fifth: when an act or an extrinsically paradoxical, or even blameworthy, work is comprehensible only in the light of its spiritual intention; such is the case, for example, of certain erotic symbolisms which *de*

---

[1] Pascal mistakenly attributed to the Jesuits the idea that "the end justifies the means"—we quote the now proverbial version—for in fact they were careful to specify: on condition that the means not be intrinsically vicious; if this reservation were not sufficient, no legitimate defense would be possible.

jure and *de facto* refer to metaphysical or mystical realities, and which owing to their ambiguity pertain to the domain of esoterism.

But let us now return to ordinary intentions: one has to beware of arguing, merely in order to sentimentally excuse an author, who after all is responsible for a blameworthy or even harmful work, that the work is acceptable because the intention was good; for that means that the defects of the work have a right to exist, and also that subjectivity takes precedence over objective reality; whereas "there is no right superior to that of the truth".

For example, one should not excuse a decadent and false art on the pretext that the intention of the artist was good since the content is religious; this would be to forget that the devil may wish to harm religion through believers who, as such, are obviously well-intentioned; thus it is not enough, in such cases, for the intention to be subjectively good, it must also be objectively so, namely in its productions; the objective quality being one of the measures of the subjective quality, hence of the intention, for "ye shall know them by their fruits".[2] We have in mind here a necessary quality of a work, not merely a desirable one; the insufficiency of a work which is merely unskillful and naive, but innocent, is not of the same order as the badness of an ill-inspired work. Clearly, the falsity of an artistic or literary production can manifest a fundamental defect: a lack of self-knowledge, an unhealthy desire for originality, hence basically pride, whatever the superficial intention of the author might be. That the latter may believe that which is bad to be good and that his intention, on this basis, may be sincere, does not constitute an extenuating circumstance, otherwise one would have to excuse all errors and all crimes, as, by the way, is done all too readily in our day.

An intention may be good in one respect and bad in another: it is good inasmuch as it manifests a religious sentiment, for example, and it is bad inasmuch as it does so in a way that, strictly speaking, is incompatible with religion, holiness, dignity. To manifest a false,

---

[2] In the religious painters of the *Quattrocento*, the intention concretely takes precedence over the execution: we do not reproach a Fra Angelico for not having been a painter of icons, given his capacity to create a quasi-paradisal climate, thus sacralizing an art that strictly speaking was already profane. On the other hand, one must not overestimate the material and even the spiritual adequateness of certain icons, since they much more often express a collective religious sentiment rather than the plenary reality of the subject represented.

stupid, or perverse mentality, is obviously to wish to do so; it is to identify oneself with this mentality, and in this respect the intention could not be good. Spontaneous, hence sincere, originality may of course be justified; but the desire for originality is never justifiable. No doubt, the desire to make something new can spur a talent, but it certainly lacks piety and also grandeur.

The fixed idea that the argument of intention is a panacea has become so habitual that too many people abuse it without reflecting, for example by protesting their good intention in cases where the question of intention could not even arise. Quite generally, it is all too clear that good intentions in no way constitute a guarantee of a man's worth, nor even, consequently, of his salvation; in this sense, intention has worth only through its actualization.[3]

Intentionism and sincerism go hand-in-hand; what the first has in common with the second is that it flies to defend all things blame-worthy, whether extravagant and pernicious or simply mediocre and vulgar; in short, to be "sincere", is to show oneself "as one is", unconditionally and cynically, hence counter to any effort to be what one ought to be. It is forgotten that the worth of sincerity lies in its contents only, and that it is charity to avoid giving a bad example; the individual owes society a correct comportment, to say the least, which has nothing to do with the vice of dissimulation. Let us specify that correct comportment, such as is required by good sense and traditional morality, has as a necessary corollary a certain effacement, whereas hypocrisy by definition is a kind of exhibitionism, crude or subtle as the case may be.

Still in connection with intentionism and sincerism, it is necessary to point out the common abuse of the word "understand", or of the notion of "understanding": we are told that one has to "understand"

---

[3] As the German, or the analogous English, proverb has it: "The road to hell is paved with good intentions" (*Der Weg zur Hölle ist mit guten Vorsätzen gepflastert*); doubtless they derive from this saying of Ecclesiasticus (21:10): "The way of sinners is made plain with stones, but at the end thereof is the pit of hell." And according to the Epistle of Saint James (4:17), "To him that knoweth to do good, and doeth it not, to him it is sin."

a lawbreaker or a bad man and that to understand is to forgive. If this were so, what is one to think of sinners who convert, and above all of the traditional injunction to "know thyself"?[4] The good thief of the Gospel did not go to Paradise for nothing, and Saint Augustine knew what he was doing when writing his *Confessions*. With a quite characteristic inconsistency, the partisans of unconditional "understanding"—it is as if it sufficed to be "me" to always be right—are careful to keep from "understanding" those who think otherwise than them, and whom they vilify shamelessly; a one-way charity necessarily ends in an upside-down justice.

Intention determines not only actions, but obviously also moral attitudes. There is a humility, a charity, and a sincerity—albeit merely in appearance—stemming from hypocrisy, hence properly from satanism, namely: egalitarian and demagogic humility, humanistic and basically bitter charity, and cynical sincerity. There are false virtues whose motives are basically to demonstrate to oneself that one has no need of God; the sin of pride consists here in believing that our virtues are our property and not a gift of Heaven; which is all the more wrong in that, in this case, the virtues are imaginary, since pride perverts them.

To be sincere, and thus to have a good intention, means among other things that one take the trouble to reflect and also, when necessary, to inform oneself, especially when a serious matter is at stake; we cannot, when pleading a good intention, justify the error of someone who judges and concludes without making use of his intelligence and could care less of what others think or know, even when they are better than he. There are people who, disdaining religions and traditional wisdoms,[5] believe they can draw everything from within themselves, for which there is logically not the slightest reason; no doubt, the sage draws everything "from within himself"—*regnum Dei intra vos est*—in the sense that he benefits from intellectual intuition; but such intuition, aside from the fact that it has nothing to do with either ambition or *a fortiori*, presumption, accords with the sacred traditions,

---

[4] Or "hate thy soul", according to a Christian formula.

[5] It is arbitrary to object that the religions contradict each other, for one can also, and with even more reason, argue that they coincide in the essential and that their antinomies in no way diminish their intrinsic efficacy. To speak of religion is to speak of Revelation, whether primordial or historical; pseudo-religions cannot be efficacious, nor any methods taken out of their traditional framework.

from which the sage does not dream of turning away, even if he is born with infused knowledge. Be that as it may, religions and wisdoms are values as "natural"—although "supernaturally" so—as the air we breathe, the water we drink, the food we eat; not to acknowledge the "categorical imperative" of what by comparison could be termed "spiritual ecology", is therefore an attitude as self-destructive as it is unrealistic.

Still in connection with the questions of intention and sincerity, but in a very particular domain, let us now consider a crucial point in initiatic "alchemy": starting from the idea that the two poles of the contemplative path are mental concentration and intention of the heart, it will easily be understood why the latter has priority over the former; for it is obviously better to have the appropriate intention without knowing how to be well concentrated than to know how to concentrate properly but without being concerned about the right intention.[6]

God listens to the intention of even an incompetent person, but He could never accept the technical perfection of the ambitious and the hypocritical. All this is said without losing sight of the fact that, in another respect, the quality of concentration depends upon the intention, precisely.

Following these parenthetical remarks, let us redescend into the arena of current and "horizontal" psychology and say a few words concerning a notion that has lent itself to scandalous abuse in the realm of psychoanalytical narcissism, namely that of "traumatism". In reality, man can only be legitimately traumatized by monstrosities; he who is traumatized by anything less than that is himself a monster; the alternative is inexorable. At any rate, a traumatism has no right to be absolute; it

---

[6] Metaphysical discernment first of all, then concentration that is sincere—because conforming to discernment—and quasi-permanent; this is the very foundation of operative spirituality, whatever might be its modes or degrees.

is there to be overcome and to be leveraged in view of that which is the reason for being of our life and of our very existence. There is no worse hypocrite than an ungrateful and spiteful man who pretends to flee towards God; God cannot be loved out of hatred for one's fellow men. Many saints had good reasons for being "traumatized", but they accepted the injustices—not imaginary in their case—"for the love of God", and without forgetting that "with what measure ye mete, it shall be measured to you again".[7]

But one has also to consider the case of collective traumatism: it is natural for a people, or some large human group, to be traumatized without there being any reason to blame them for it; and again, it is just as natural that this would not involve every individual. A collective soul is passive, and it is necessarily so since it can have neither a homogeneous intelligence nor the free and precise will that stems from it; this is one more reason not to allow oneself to be dominated by a collective psychism and not to grant it power. Although passive, the collectivity can nonetheless be the vehicle of a good disposition, depending on its mental and moral health combined with the tradition; *vox populi, vox Dei.*

Let us return once more to the question of sincerity: it is not astonishing that for the sincerism in vogue nowadays, secrecy is detestable since, from this point of view, to be sincere is to hide nothing, and thus to hide something is to be dishonest or hypocritical. Now for obvious reasons, man has a natural right to secrecy: he has the right not to show a feeling or *a fortiori* a spiritual grace that concerns only himself;[8] a saint may wish to conceal, if not his virtues, at least his sanctity. Sincerity thus consists less in showing in every respect what one is, than in not wishing to appear to be more than one is—which a dignitary invested with a social or spiritual function could not be blamed for, since his normative demeanor refers to the principle he represents and not to his individuality. For the mentality of "our times" on the

---

[7] A classic example is Saint John of the Cross, always persecuted and in the end canonized; but never "traumatized", to say the least.

[8] "Neither cast ye your pearls before swine", said Christ.

contrary, to be vulgar is to be sincere and inversely, which presupposes the opinion that man is normally vulgar; as a result, vulgarity has become quasi-official. Be that as it may, dignity stems from piety, from reverential fear, as well as from love; even the sinner has the right to visible dignity, which is to say that dignity is incumbent upon him because he is a human being, "made in the image of God", despite his insufficiency or betrayal. Certainly, there are perverse men who affect worthy manners—impostors, for example—but they do so for false reasons, hence out of hypocrisy; true dignity could not be affected, it is sincere by definition. Man is noble to the extent that he identifies with the principial and thus with the necessary; with the archetype and not with the accident.

From all that we have just said it follows that the man of "aristocratic" nature—we are not speaking of social classes—is he who masters himself and who loves to master himself; the "plebeian" by nature—with the same reservation[9]—is on the contrary he who does not master himself, and who does not wish to do so. To master oneself is in substance to want to transcend oneself, in conformity with the reason for being of that central and total creature which is man; in fact, the man of the "dark age" lives below himself. Thus, he must transcend himself—or reestablish the equilibrium between *Māyā* and *Ātmā*—in accordance with a norm which he bears within himself, and which entails all that makes life worth living.

All told, the main question is to know what we are, or what man is; now our true identity is in our consciousness of the Real, of the Immutable, of the Sovereign Good. All psychological, moral, social, and spiritual anthropology has to have its foundation in this axiom; it follows that to defend man is above all to defend him against himself.

To resume our initial subject, we shall again specify, at the risk of repeating ourselves, that intention comprises essentially two dimensions, or that it operates in two phases: firstly, the good ought to be

---

[9] All the more so in that the social classes have become largely artificial owing to destructive, dehumanizing, and enslaving industrialism. The phenomenon of aristocratic peasants and craftsmen, above all in regions that are still fully religious, should be well known.

done, and secondly, it ought to be well done. To accomplish something good is also to accomplish it well, for the execution ought to be up to the idea; this is what sincerity as well as logic demand. As we have seen above, "right doing" also comprises, in principle if not always in fact, formal language, or let us say the mode of expression of the execution.

Another fundamental point is the emphasis, either of the intention or of the action; an excessive legalism will see in correct action a gauge of merit and virtue, whereas a unitive mysticism[10] will tend to see in outward observances a formalism that is either secondary or even superfluous; rightly or wrongly depending on the case, or depending on the spiritual scope of the subject. In principle, the second attitude is more important than the first because the inward has priority over the outward, or because, precisely, intention takes precedence over action; but in this case the intention at issue is an intrinsic one, that is to say, sufficing unto itself and concretely encompassing the possibilities of meritorious action.[11] From Christ's standpoint, the observance of a prescription is obligatory only on the twofold condition that the prescription adequately express its reason for being and that man, in acting, realize this reason for being in his soul; as King David said (40:6, 8): "Sacrifice and offering thou didst not desire; mine ears hast thou opened . . . thy law is within my heart."

---

[10] This expression should be understood in the widest sense, including *gnosis* as well as the way of love; *jnāna* as well as *bhakti*.

[11] The distinction "intention-action" evokes the complementary relationship between "faith" and "works". The speculative and operative divergences that these two principles have given rise to in the East as well as in the West are well-known.

Remarks on Charity

The word "charity" signifies goodness that makes itself known, goodness in action. Theologically, by charity is meant the love of God and neighbor; in ordinary language, the word charity, considered in isolation, means beneficial action in relation to those who need it; but in certain contexts, this word also means: to be considerate of others' feelings. Thus, it is commonly said: "Out of charity, do not tell him that, it could make him sad", or: "Be good enough to please him in this way"; all of which has nothing to do with caring for the sick or with giving alms.

When charitableness is reproached for being accompanied by an "excessive indulgence" or by a "condescension", this reproach has in view merely a sentimental contingency that is difficult to measure and largely uncertain; for "let not thy left hand know what thy right hand doeth", and elementary virtue has always required that charity be done as modestly as possible. Thus, it suffices to keep this in mind; and this has no connection with the concept as such of charity, seeing that charity itself requires that it be exercised charitably, hence modestly.

On the other hand, if he who receives feels humiliated or wounded by the obvious inequality that all charity comprises, it is very often because he is proud, and not because the benefactor demonstrates any conceit. In our time of systematic and intensive demagoguery, one has to be skeptical with regard to gratuitous and hypersensitive protestations of "human dignity". If the benefactor has to make an effort to be modest, the beneficiary of the good deed must in his turn make an effort not to take offense; virtue is needed on both sides! If it is necessary to "educate" someone, it is necessary to educate the poor man as well as the rich, above all when the fault of the former is more serious than that of the latter, which in our time is all too frequently the case.

In charity there can be no "equal partners" since the one who helps or gives does so freely; if he does not do so freely, there is no charity. If someone collapses on the street, it is not an act of charity to help him; it is a human duty. Similarly, when someone suffers from hunger, it is a duty to feed him; but the degree of our help is a question of charity, for in this evaluation we are free. Each time there is a possible choice in the degree of our charitable intervention, there is freedom on our part and there is inequality between him who gives and him who receives; this is what proves the duty of gratitude on the part of the latter.

What has to be eliminated is not the nature of things, that is, no natural element—material or psychological—of charity, but solely the sentimental abuses that have been blamed since time immemorial. One has to beware of turning the beneficiary of charity into an insolent protestor, incapable of appreciating another's generosity; the man who does not know how to say "thank you" wholeheartedly, and without concerning himself with the psychology of his benefactor, is a monster.

Moreover, "partnerism" in charity coincides with the abolition of respect for all superiority; in a world in which each person believes himself to be the equal of everyone else in every respect, there is assuredly no place for free, hence generous and authentic, charity.[1]

We have been told that instead of relieving poverty, one has to teach men how to escape it; now, this aspect of charity is extremely limited, for the causes of poverty can be in the lack of technical skills; they can also be in the incapacity to manage money, or even in laziness; this is to say that they are moral as well as material. Besides, the meaning of the word "poverty" is quite relative, for in our day the term is used for economic situations that are doubtless primitive, but in themselves altogether normal and satisfying, and it is done with the underlying thought of finding new outlets for industrial products, which is not very charitable; needs are created in order to find buyers, and to find them it is necessary, on the one hand, to make real or fictitious poor people believe that the non-satisfaction of these needs is poverty and, on the other hand, to teach them how to go about making money. All of which is far from charity, whatever be the phraseology and the euphemisms; and which, in too many cases, is even rather far from efficacy and concrete good.

Charity is to freely, and really, help those who need and deserve it.

---

[1] We have heard it said that the traditional conception of charity is false because it implies a hierarchy, which is monstrous since hierarchy, and with it inequality, are to be found everywhere in the world and result from the very nature of Being.

No Initiative without Truth

At the beginning of this century, hardly anyone knew that the world was ailing—authors like Guénon and Coomaraswamy were preaching in the desert—whereas nowadays, almost everyone knows this; but it is far from the case that everyone knows the root cause of the ailment and is capable of discerning the remedies. In our time one often hears that to fight against materialism, technocracy, and pseudo-spiritualism, what is needed is a new ideology, capable of resisting all seductions and all assaults, and of galvanizing those of good will. Now, the need for an ideology, or the desire to oppose one ideology to another, is already an admission of weakness, and all initiatives stemming from this prejudice are false and doomed to fail. What must be done is to counter false ideologies with the truth that has always been and that we could never invent, since it exists outside us and above us. The present world is obsessed by the bias towards dynamism, as if it were a "categorical imperative" and a panacea, and as if dynamism were meaningful and efficacious outside truth pure and simple.[1]

No man in possession of his faculties could have the intention of substituting one error for another, whether "dynamic" or not; before speaking of strength and efficacy, one ought to speak of truth and nothing else. A truth is efficacious to the extent that we assimilate it; if it does not give us the strength we need, this merely proves we have not grasped it. It is not for the truth to be "dynamic", it is for us to be dynamic thanks to the truth. What is lacking in today's world is a penetrating and comprehensive knowledge of the nature of things; fundamental truths are always accessible, but they cannot become an imperative for those who refuse to take them into consideration.

It goes without saying that what is in question here are not the wholly outward data which experimental science can provide us, but realities that this science cannot handle, and which are transmitted to us by altogether different channels, especially those of mythological and

---

[1] In popular language this is called "putting the cart before the horse". We recall that, during an economic crisis—which occurred a long time ago—there was talk of "creating a mystique of recovery"; as if the calamities of industrialism were imaginary maladies, curable through autosuggestion, and as if autosuggestion could transform subjective chimeras into objective realities.

metaphysical symbolism, not to mention intellectual intuition, which resides as a principial possibility in every man. The symbolic language of the great traditions of mankind may seem difficult and disconcerting for certain minds, but it is nevertheless intelligible in the light of the orthodox commentaries; symbolism, it must be stressed, is a real and rigorous science, and nothing is more aberrant than to believe that its apparent naivety issues from a rudimentary and "prelogical" mentality. This science, which can be qualified as "sacred", cannot be adapted to the experimental method of the moderns; the domain of revelation, of symbolism, of pure intellection obviously transcends the physical and psychic planes and therefore is situated beyond the domain of methods termed scientific. If we believe that we cannot accept the language of traditional symbolism because it seems to us fantastic and arbitrary, this only shows that we have not yet understood this language, but certainly not that we have gone beyond it.

It is rather convenient to claim, as is so speciously done in our day, that religions have compromised themselves over the course of centuries and that their role has now ended. When one knows what a religion really consists of, one also knows that the religions cannot compromise themselves and that they are independent from human abuses; in fact, nothing men do has the power to affect traditional doctrines, symbols, and rites, so long of course as human activities remain on their own level and do not attack sacred things. The fact that an individual may exploit religion in order to bolster up national or private interests in no wise affects religion in its capacity as message and patrimony.

Tradition speaks to each man the language he can understand, provided he be willing to listen; this reservation is essential, for tradition, we repeat, cannot become "bankrupt"; it is rather of man's bankruptcy that one should speak, for it is he who has lost the intuition of the supernatural and the sense of the sacred. Man has allowed himself to be seduced by the discoveries and inventions of an illegitimately totalitarian science; that is, a science which does not recognize its own limits and for that reason is unaware of what lies beyond them. Fascinated by scientific phenomena as well as by the erroneous conclusions he draws from them, man has ended up being submerged by his own creations; he is not ready to realize that a traditional message is situated on an altogether different level, and how much more real this level is. Men let themselves be dazzled all the more readily since scientism gives them all the excuses they want to justify their attachment to the world of appearances and thus also their flight before the presence of the Absolute in any form.

Spinozist, deist, Kantian, and freemasonic humanism intended to achieve a perfect man outside the truths that give the human phenomenon all its meaning.[2] As it was of course necessary to replace one God by another, this false idealism gave rise to the abuse of intelligence characteristic of the nineteenth century, especially to scientism and with it industrialism; the latter in its turn brought about a new ideology, one equally flat and explosive, namely the paradoxically inhuman humanism that is Marxism. The internal contradiction of Marxism is that it wants to build a perfect humanity while destroying man; which is to say that militant atheists, more impassioned than realistic, wish to overlook that religion is so to speak a question of ecology. Assuming that religion comprises an element of "opium"—not solely "for the people"—this element is "ecologically" indispensable for the human psychism; its absence, at any rate, brings about incomparably worse abuses than its presence, for it is better to have good dreams than to have nightmares. Be that as it may, only religion, or spirituality, offers that integral meaning and happiness anchored in man's deiform nature, without which life is neither intelligible nor worth living.

A facile argument against religions is the following: the religions and denominations contradict one another, hence they cannot all be right; consequently, none is true. It is as if one were to say: every individual claims to be "I", hence they cannot all be right; consequently, no one is "I"; all of which amounts to asserting that there is but one single man to see the mountain and that the mountain has but a single side to be seen. Only traditional metaphysics does justice to the rigor of objectivity and to the rights of subjectivity; it alone is capable of explaining the unanimity of the sacred doctrines as well as their formal divergences.

---

[2] A humanism that could be termed "pre-atheism" since it prepared the ground for, or opened the door to, atheism properly so called.

"When the inferior man hears about the *Tao*, he laughs at it; it would not be the *Tao* if he did not laugh at it. . . . The self-evidence of the *Tao* is taken for darkness." These words of Lao Tzu are more timely than ever; no doubt, errors and stupidities cannot but be as long as their altogether relative possibility has not been exhausted; but they are certainly not the ones that will have the final word.

A point that we would like to stress at the risk of repeating ourselves is this: one readily speaks of the duty of being useful to society, but one fails to ask whether this society itself is useful, that is to say whether it realizes man's, and thus a human community's, reason for being; quite clearly, if the individual must be useful to the collectivity, the latter for its part must be useful to the individual. The human quality implies that the collectivity could not be the aim and reason for being of the individual, but on the contrary that it is the individual, in his solitary station before the Absolute and thus by the exercise of his highest function, who is the aim and reason for being of the collectivity. Man, whether conceived in the plural or the singular, is like a "fragment of absoluteness" and is made for the Absolute; he has no other choice. The social can be defined in terms of the truth, but the truth cannot be defined in terms of the social.

These considerations lead us to the pointlessly controversial question of "altruism": there are "idealists", in India as in the West—as seen in the sentimentalism of a Vivekananda—who readily blame "those who seek their own salvation" instead of concerning themselves with saving others; an absurd alternative, for one of two things must hold true: either it is possible to save others, or it is impossible to do so; if it is possible, this implies that we first seek our personal salvation, otherwise saving others is impossible, precisely; in any case, to remain placidly attached to one's own faults does no one a favor. He who is capable of becoming a saint but neglects to become one cannot save anyone; it is hypocrisy pure and simple to hide one's own weakness and lukewarmness behind a screen of good works. Another error, related to the one just mentioned, consists in believing that contemplative spirituality is opposed to action or renders man incapable of acting; an opinion belied by all the Scriptures, notably the *Bhagavad Gītā*.

No initiative outside the truth: this is the first principle of action, without however being a guarantee of success; still, man must do his duty without asking whether he will be victorious or not, for faithfulness to principles has its own intrinsic value; it bears its fruit in itself and means *ipso facto* a victory in the soul of the agent. We are in the "iron age", and outward victory cannot come about except through a divine intervention; nonetheless, logically and spiritually correct activity can have incalculable effects, or at least partial effects, outside us as well as within us.

Being Conscious of the Real

The purpose of human intelligence, and consequently the purpose of man, is the consciousness of the Absolute, not only beyond but also within the consciousness of contingencies. If its purpose is to seek distraction in futilities, or to lead an antlike existence, then it was not worth being born into the human state, and the phenomenon of human intelligence—reduced to a pointless luxury—would be inexplicable.

In connection with man's vocation, it is necessary to understand Saint Anselm's ontological argument correctly: it does not mean that the capacity to imagine no matter what proves the existence of the thing imagined; it means that the capacity to conceive God proves a spiritual scope that can be explained only by the reality of God. According to the same Doctor, faith comes before knowledge (*credo ut intelligam*); in short, faith is presented here as the qualification for intellection, which is to say that in order to be able to understand, one has to possess the sense of the transcendent and of the sacred. But the converse is also true: "I understand that I may believe" (*intelligo ut credam*)—which no one has ever said—could mean that before possessing a quasi-existential certitude of transcendent realities, it is important to grasp the doctrine. In a certain respect, the predisposition of the heart is the key to metaphysical truth reflected in the mind; in another respect, this conceptual knowledge is the key to the science of the heart.

"Blessed are they that have not seen, and yet have believed": it is a question here of the outer man, immersed in the maze of phenomena. Faith is the intuition of the transcendent; unbelief stems from the layer of ice that covers the heart and excludes this intuition. In mystical language, the human heart is either "liquid" or "hardened"; it has also been compared to a mirror that is either polished or rusted. "They that have believed": they who place the intuition of the supernatural above a way of reasoning that is servile and cut off from its roots.

— ∴ —

We have said that man's vocation is the consciousness of the Absolute; the parable of the persistent widow and the unjust judge reminds us that this consciousness, which is "now", ought to be "always", which is to say that its very content demands totality; it must be "always" lest it be "never". However, to "pray without ceasing", as Saint Paul wishes, could not imply a perfect continuity, unrealizable in earthly life; in fact, perseverance works through rhythms—rigorous or approximate—and it is these that serve as perpetuity. The inevitable gaps between spiritual acts are recipients of grace—the angels do for us what we cannot do—so that the life of prayer suffers no discontinuity.

Nothing gives us the right to forget the Essential; certainly, our earthly existence is woven of pleasures and labors, joys and sorrows, hopes and fears, but all that is without common measure with the consciousness of the Absolute and with our quasi-ontological duty to practice it. "Let the dead bury their dead", said Christ, and he added: "And follow me"; namely, in the direction of the "kingdom of God which is within you".[1]

In order to be thus faithful to ourselves we have need of indisputable arguments: of keys allowing us to remain in the consciousness of the Sovereign Good despite the troubles of the world and of the soul. The fundamental argument is that "*Brahman* is real, the world is illusory" (*Brahma satyam jagan mithyā*), which cuts short all the wiles of the earthly *māyā*; doubtless, this argument is one of the most demanding, both intellectually and psychologically, in the sense that it presupposes a concrete intuition of the Real and not merely an abstract idea; it must therefore be accompanied by other key ideas, closer to our earthly and daily experience.

On the plane of our human relationship with God, the first indispensable argument is the evidence that the world cannot be other than what it is and that we cannot change it; hence that we must resign ourselves to that which cannot but be, and resist all temptation—even unconscious—to revolt against destiny and against the nature of things; this is what is called "accepting the will of Heaven". To the quality of resignation is joined that of trust; the Divinity is substan-

---

[1] The same meaning is found in this saying: "But thou, when thou prayest, enter into thy closet, and when thou hast shut thy door, pray to thy Father which is in secret. . .". Similarly again: "No man, having put his hand to the plough, and looking back, is fit for the kingdom of God."

tially benevolent, its intrinsic goodness precedes its quasi-accidental rigor; to be conscious of this is to dwell in peace and to know that all things are in God's hands.

In many cases, it matters little that our right be safeguarded; egoism—or let us say, the bias of not being able to bear any injustice—is a serious pitfall in our relationship with Heaven, and that is why Christ prescribed loving one's enemies[2] and turning the other cheek. In a word, one has to know how to forget oneself before God and in view of our last ends, all the more so as in the final analysis it is only in this climate of detachment that we can have access to the certitude, both transcendent and immanent, that "the soul is not other than *Brahman*" (*jivo brahmaiva nāparah*).[3]

To the qualities of resignation and trust ought to be joined that of gratitude: quite often, the remembrance of the good things we enjoy—and which others may not enjoy—can attenuate a trial and contribute to the serenity demanded by the consciousness of the Absolute. Another argument, finally, is based on our freedom: we are free to do what we want to do, to be what we want to be; no seduction or trial can prevent us from having recourse to the saving consciousness of the Sovereign Good.

—— ·:· ——

In our consciousness of God, our desire for liberation meets the will of God to free us; prayer is at once a question and a response. If "beauty is the splendor of the true", the same can be said of goodness; if the good tends to communicate itself, that is because it also tends to liberate us.

Christ's injunction to "love God with all thy heart, with all thy soul, with all thy strength, and with all thy mind", reminds us that the consciousness of the Absolute is absolute: that we cannot know and love That which alone is, except with all that we are. The unicity of the object demands the totality of the subject; this indicates that in the

[2] This is the condemnation, not of the defense of a vital right, but of excess in the defense of that right; justice is not vengeance.

[3] A consciousness that on the one hand transcends the ego and on the other belongs to its transpersonal essence.

last analysis the object and the subject rejoin in pure Reality, which is at once the undifferentiated Essence and ultimate Cause, hence the Source of all differentiation. To speak of the Absolute is to speak of the Infinite, and consequently manifestation and diversity; and the projection of the Good implies ontologically the return to the Good.

—— .:. ——

Discernment and contemplation; concentration and perseverance; resignation and trust; humility and charity. Spirituality is what man is: being made of intelligence, will, and sentiment—all three faculties having the principial quality of objectivity on pain of not being human—spirituality has as its constitutive elements the Truth, the Way, and Virtue—Virtue giving rise to the two complementary poles of humility and charity, precisely. The Way is attached to the Truth; Virtue is attached to both the Truth and the Way.

Humility prolongs—in moral mode—the element Truth or Knowledge because Knowledge teaches us the proportions of things; man could not know metaphysical Reality without first knowing himself. Charity, for its part, prolongs the element Way or Realization because this element essentially requires Grace; man could not deserve mercy without being merciful himself. He who raises himself unduly will be abased, and he who abases himself—in conformity with the nature of things—will be raised; and this through participation in the elevation of the Real. And similarly: he who unjustly rejects his neighbor will be rejected by God, and he who accepts his neighbor— in conformity with justice and generosity—will be accepted by God, that is to say by Him who is hidden in the "neighbor" in virtue of the omnipresence of the Self. It will be understood that charity refers more particularly to immanence, and humility to transcendence.

A priori, metaphysics is abstract; but it would not be what it is if it did not give rise *a posteriori* to concrete prolongations on the plane of our human and earthly existence. The Real encompasses all that is; the consciousness of the Real entails all that we are.

The Liberating Passage

From the perspective of transcendence, there is quite evidently a discontinuity between the divine Principle and its manifestation; but from the point of view of immanence, there is continuity. According to the first relationship, we shall say "manifestation and not Principle"; according to the second, "manifested Principle, hence still Principle". When there is discontinuity, we distinguish between the Essence and the form; when there is continuity, we distinguish between the Substance and the accident. In both cases, there is Reality and the veil; Absoluteness and relativity.

In order to be less abstract, let us specify that the accident is to the Substance what ice or steam is to water, and that the form is to the Essence what the reflection is to the sun; or again, on quite a different plane: the relationship between the participle and the verb equals that of the accident and the Substance, and the relationship between the word and the thing signified equals that between the form and the Essence. And similarly, on the spiritual plane: when we distinguish between the symbol and its principial archetype, the "Idea" (*Eidos*),[1] we refer to the discontinuous and static relationship "form-Essence"; but when we distinguish between the rite and its effect, we refer to the relationship "accident-Substance", which is continuous and dynamic. This is to say that the accident is a "mode" of the Substance, whereas the form is a "sign" of the Essence.[2]

Every sacred symbol is an "enlightening form" that invites to a "liberating rite"; the "form" reveals the Essence to us, whereas the "rite" leads us back to the Substance; to the Substance we are, the only one that is. All this concerns sacred art and "liturgy", on the one hand, and the beauties of nature, on the other; it also concerns, with all the more reason, the symbolism of concepts and the rites of assimilation. Vision of the Essence through the form, and return to the Substance by means of the rite.

---

[1] Or the "Paradigm", which is the Idea viewed in its aspect of initial Norm or celestial Ideal. We use capital letters when it is a question of the divine Order, even though we fear overusing them.

[2] Nonetheless, the terms "substance" and "essence" are synonymous inasmuch as they simply designate the archetypal content of a phenomenon.

There is the visual symbol and the auditory symbol, then the enacted symbol, all of which enable the passage from the outward to the Inward, from the accident to the Substance, and thereby also the passage from the form to the Essence.[3] Let us take the opportunity here to point out that a noble and profound person tends to see the Substance in the accidents, whereas an inferior person sees only the accidents and tends to reduce the substantial manifestations to a trivializing accidentality. The sense of the sacred and of the celestial is the measure of human worth.[4]

— .:. —

Hence, when contrasting the notions of "form" and "essence", it will be said that there is discontinuity; when contrasting the notions of "accident" and "substance", it will be said on the contrary that there is continuity. But when one considers, on the one hand, the conformation of the form to the essence and, on the other, the manifestation of the essence in the form, or when one considers—and this amounts in practice to the same thing—the conformation of the accident to the substance and the manifestation of the substance in the accident, the question of discontinuity or continuity does not arise. For conformation, which is "ascending", just as that of manifestation, which is "descending", are altogether independent of the distinction in question.

The divine symbol, by definition, is paradoxically ambiguous: on the one hand it "is God"—that is its reason for being—and on the other it "is not God"—that is its earthly materiality; it is "image" because it is manifestation and not Principle, and it is participating emanation and liberating sacrament because it is *Ātmā* in *Māyā*. The human body in itself—not in a given diminished form—is a symbol-sacrament because it is "made in the image of God"; that is why it is the object of love *par excellence*; not to the exclusion of the

[3] In a particularly direct way, music and dance are supports for a passage—at whatever degree—from the accident to the Substance; and this is above all the meaning of rhythm. The same is true of sacred nudity and all contemplative recourse to virgin nature, the primordial sanctuary.

[4] Which cuts short the hasty and barbarous distinction between the "savage" and the "civilized".

soul that dwells in it, but together with this soul, for the human body has its form only in virtue of the content for which it is made. The body invites to adoration by its very theomorphic form, and that is why it can be the vehicle of a celestial presence that in principle is salvific; but, as Plato suggests, this presence is accessible only to the contemplative soul not dominated by passion, and quite apart from the question of knowing whether the person is an ascetic or is married. Sexuality does not mean animality, except in perverted, hence sub-human, man; in the properly human man, sexuality is determined by that which constitutes man's prerogative, as is attested, precisely, by the theomorphic form of his body.

And this leads us back to our distinction between the Essence and the Substance: the masculine pole refers to essentiality and transcendence, and the feminine pole to substantiality and immanence. The trajectory towards the Sovereign Good—which is at once the Absolute and the Infinite—necessarily comprises modes that are so to speak masculine as well as feminine; *a priori* and *grosso modo*, the Truth pertains to Rigor and to Justice, and the Path to Gentleness and to Mercy. In loving woman, man essentially loves Infinitude and Goodness; woman, in loving man, essentially loves Absoluteness and Strength; the Universe being woven of geometry and musicality, of strength and beauty.

Transcendence—we have said above—means discontinuity between the Principle and its manifestation, hence separation, and immanence means continuity, hence union; thus it is that divine Virility, with the implacability of the nature of things, imposes upon us principles that derive from the Immutable, and that divine Femininity, on the contrary, with all the freedom that Love disposes of, grants us the imponderable graces that bring about the miracle of Salvation.

APPENDIX

Selections from Letters and
Other Previously Unpublished Writings

1

The Supreme Reality, which for man is the Sovereign Good, attracts us in three ways: through Truth, through Salvation, through Beauty.

Attraction through Truth presupposes, on the part of man, an intelligence that is penetrating and profound; attraction through Salvation demands a will that is strong and persevering; attraction through Beauty takes place thanks to a soul that is noble and contemplative.

For certain people, the point of departure is the intelligence, hence Truth. For others, the point of departure is the desire for Salvation—or simply the fear of falling into hell—whence an emphasis on the element will. For others again, the point of departure is nobility and depth of soul, hence Beauty. But it goes without saying that these three viewpoints can, and must, be combined; this is in the logic of things, whatever the individual emphases may be.

The exoterisms insist perforce on the elements Salvation and will; the elements Truth and intelligence, Beauty and nobility, belong—regarding what is quintessential and decisive in them—to the esoteric dimension. This, however, in nowise alters the fact that beneath the veil of every exoterism the esoteric elements can, and even must, reveal themselves.

2

The beloved is the mirror of the one who loves; each of the two acts as a spiritual stimulant for the other, the spiritual modality of the beloved—quite apart from the degree of knowledge—always acting, by definition, as a symbolic ideal for the one who loves; it is thus since beings love each other in virtue of their complementarism, spiritual as well as psychic and corporeal, the body being but the outward expression of the spiritual aspect. It is the idea, the truth, or the knowledge, manifested by man, that stimulates the woman's spirituality, and it is the faith, the conformity, or the virtue, manifested by woman, that stimulates the man's spirituality; one can also say that man manifests intelligence and strength, whereas woman manifests goodness and beauty, and that their union brings about the Adamic plenitude which, for its part, is made in "the image of God", as is taught in Genesis; this too is the meaning of this Arab proverb: "The beauty of man lies in his intelligence and the intelligence of woman lies in her beauty." According to Ibn Arabi, the Prophet loved his wives as God loves His Creation, and his wives loved him as he loved *Allāh*; thus man and woman have a love that is respectively particular to each; but love in itself, such as we have described it, does not apply to the individual as a sexual being, but as a human being, the quality of humanness being more real than the quality of man or of woman, and the quality of human love being more important than masculine or feminine love.

3

There are four fundamental expressions of human beauty: 1. The formal structure of the face; with it the natural, psychic expression; and above all the supra-natural, spiritual expression. 2. The body. 3. The movements of the body; dancing. 4. The gestures of the hands; the *mūdra*s.

Beauty of the face expresses, not an actual perfection of the personality, but a possibility of Perfection. In French one says: *noblesse oblige*—which implies: if God gave you a seed, it must give back, to God and to yourselves, a fruit. As to the beauty of the body, it expresses, first Divine Manifestation as such; and second, the harmony of this manifestation. The movements of the body express what we could call the life of this manifestation; for the universal complement of statism is dynamism. The hands, and especially the gestures, exteriorize the spiritual capacities and functions of the personality—made in the image of God.

4

Man is *pontifex* by definition, which means that he lives in two completely different dimensions; this is the Eckhartian distinction between the outer man and the inner man. First of all, we stand before God, and this situation has something absolute about it; then, we live in the world of phenomena, and this situation—woven of relativities—is determined by the preceding one. The result of this incommensurability is that when we look towards God—when we invoke Him—all the noise of earthly *māyā* is shut out; it is thus sufficient that we know that everything is in God's hands; our forgetting of the world equals trust in God. A Koranic sentence teaches us to "Say *Allāh*! and leave them to their vain discourse"; this "vain discourse" is our thoughts and the worldly matters that provoke them. The best way to master life's problems is to forget them in the face of God, while putting them in His hands; this forgetting, I repeat, is synonymous with trust. Life is complicated, but we must simplify it by means of the absolute element I have just mentioned; we must not give way to the vertigo of phenomena. We must realize an equilibrium between the outer and the inner, the horizontal and the vertical; this equilibrium is man's vocation. *Et in terra pax hominibus bonae voluntatis.*

5

A phenomenon, whatever it may be, exists because it is a possibility, whether we understand it or not; when it touches us, for good or for ill, it is a destiny. Each phenomenon of which we are aware offers itself to our sensibility and to our intelligence as a possibility, and inserts itself into our life as destiny, if only to a minute degree. The awareness that we have of a far-off, or some past, or insignificant thing enters into our destiny as much as our awareness of something near and actual, and possibly important.

When we encounter the absurd, we must say to ourselves at the outset that it is a possibility and that the meeting with it is destined; one must accept the possibility of the absurd—of error or of injustice or of incoherence or of deception for example—before having grasped the cause or the mechanism of the phenomenon; for it suffices *a priori* to know that the absurd enters necessarily into the economy of *Māyā*, and in consequence also into that of a human life. One must accuse neither the world nor life—this would be, indirectly, to accuse God, *quod absit*—and one must absolutely avoid the pitfalls of melancholy and bitterness, which stem from ignorance and egoism, even stupidity and pride. This is not to say that man does not have the right to traumatisms, at least not to those which establish themselves in the soul as a legitimate acquisition, precisely; for man has a certain very relative right to natural weaknesses, to the extent that he seeks to vanquish them. Natural weakness is only an attenuating circumstance in one who is faithful to the human vocation, of which the alpha and omega is God.

6

To cut off man from the Absolute and reduce him to a collective phenomenon is to deprive him of all right to existence *qua* man. If man deserves that so many efforts should be spent on his behalf, this cannot be simply because he exists, eats, and sleeps or because he likes what is pleasant and hates what is unpleasant, for the lowest of the animals share this same modality without therefore being considered our equals and deserving to be treated accordingly. To the objection that man is distinguished from the animals by his intelligence, we will answer that it is precisely this intellectual superiority that the social egalitarianism of the moderns fails to take into account, so much so that an argument which is not applied consistently to men cannot then be turned against the animals. To the objection that man is distinguished from animals by his "culture" we will answer that the completely profane and worldly "culture" in question is nothing more than a specifically dated pastime of the human animal; that is to say, this culture can be anything one pleases, while waiting for the human animal to suppress it altogether. The capacity for absoluteness characterizing human intelligence is the only thing conferring on man a right of primacy; it is only this capacity that gives him the right to harness a horse to a cart. Tradition, by its otherworldly character, manifests the real superiority of man; tradition alone is a "humanism" in the positive sense of the word. Anti-traditional culture, by the very fact that it is without the sense of the Absolute and even the sense of truth—for these two things go together—could never confer on man that unconditional value and those indisputable rights which modern humanitari-anism attributes to him *a priori* and without any logical justification.

The same could also be expressed in another way: When people speak of "culture", they generally think of a host of contingencies, of a thousand ways of uselessly agitating the mind and dispersing one's attention, but they do not think of that principle which alone con-fers lawfulness on human works; this principle is the transcendent truth, whence springs all genuine culture. It is impossible to defend a culture effectively without referring it back to its spiritual principle and without seeking therein the sap that supports life. Agreement between cultures means agreement on spiritual principles; for truth, despite great differences of expression, remains one.

7

Regarding the subject you intend to treat in your book, my perspec-tive is of course very different from that of psychologists and other empiricists. Proceeding from the idea that the absolutely Real is essentially Being, Consciousness, and Beatitude, and accepting that the Real, due to its very infinity, produces relativity and consequently a multitude of reverberations, I see in the human soul a reflection of absolute Consciousness, one determined by a fabric of cosmic con-tingencies. Now since by definition the human soul is commensurate with the Absolute—which is its *raison d'être* and the sole explanation for its characteristic faculties—man is made for transcendence, which explains the religious phenomenon and all spiritualities.

8

All the traditional doctrines agree in this: from a strictly spiritual point of view, though not necessarily from other much more relative and therefore less important points of view, mankind is becoming more and more corrupted; the ideas of "evolution", of "progress", and of a single "civilization" are in effect the most pernicious pseudo-dogmas the world has ever produced, for there is no newfound error that does not eagerly attach its own claims to the above beliefs. We say not that evolution is nonexistent, but that it has a partial and most often a quite external applicability; if there is evolution on the one hand, there are degenerations on the other, and it is in any case radically false to suppose that our ancestors were intellectually, spiritually, or morally our inferiors. To suppose this is the most childish of "optical delusions"; human weakness alters its style in the course of history, but not its nature.

9

Metaphysical certitude is not God. Man must always count, not only on God, who determines him and on whom everything depends, but also on the divine Will, which concerns human, earthly, and cosmic facts in a particular manner. Thus, man depends on the Divinity in two ways: firstly, inasmuch as he is man, manifestation, and creature, and secondly, inasmuch as he acts; and man must devote himself to God in two respects: firstly, that of existence, and secondly, that of action. To be through God and for God; to want what He wants; to annihilate oneself in the root and in the fruits. Only in this way is man fully man; and it is only by being fully man that he can "realize God". "Deification" is for man, not for the human animal.

10

When one is exceptionally gifted in a spiritual sense, it can happen that one's human reality is not on the level of these gifts, and this discrepancy manifests itself paradoxically and painfully in certain circumstances, which then constitute a real trial; now one must accept the repercussions and consequences of this disharmony without being surprised by it, and above all avoid being offended or too easily wounded by it. In the spiritual life, one must "jump over one's own shadow", for the person that we are in reality, that we are in our substance—by the grace of God—is someone that we rarely are *a priori*. There is someone in ourselves that must be delivered from ourselves; that is why, from the point of view of susceptibility, we must look at ourselves from the outside as it were, as if the habitual "I" were a stranger. The whole question is knowing "who" we are, that is to say: who is "ourselves". In other words, the spiritual man is condemned to overcome himself, and much more so perhaps than he can conceive of beforehand; it is appropriate therefore not to be too sensitive about a "oneself" that is not yet sufficiently defined. All of this may be obvious, but spiritual teachings are woven of evident truths, precisely.

11

The story of Hamlet is the drama of a man who lives in two dimensions and who is so to speak torn between them, namely the ordinary human vision of things and the vision of the cosmos in its totality. Hamlet is at once a chivalrous, sensitive soul and a metaphysical and contemplative intelligence; in other words, and this is what characterizes him, he does not know how to concretely reconcile "action" and "contemplation", the demands of human sensibility and the consciousness of the vanity of all things. This is what explains his famous "hesitation" and also his profound pessimism; he wants to act, but at the same time he sees himself from above, as an actor, he sees his human role in all its contingency and all its futility; he knows that he cannot change either men or the world.

Hamlet should act and would like to act, but it is as if he has two souls, that of a prince who would like to act with justice—not base vengeance—and that of a contemplative who finds himself hypnotized by Solomonian wisdom: "Vanity of vanities.... What profit hath a man of all his labor which he taketh under the sun? . . . The thing that hath been, it is that which shall be; and that which is done is that which shall be done: and there is no new thing under the sun".

This is in any case one important aspect of Shakespeare's play.

12

Concentration appears *a priori* as a pure abstraction, as a sacred emptiness which excludes all that is not God: hence as something purely negative. Now we know that the content and reason for being of concentration is the Sovereign Good, namely that Infinitude which contains all that we have the right to love, hence all that is lovable in itself: and which contains all this because it prefigures it. And that is why one can say of concentration: "I am black, but beautiful."

In the final analysis, concentration coincides with the heart and consequently with the deepest certitude, that which includes both the Absolute and our own being. That is why it is not simply contraction; it is also dilation, peace, serenity.

It is worth recalling here that concentration can be perfect without being persevering, and that it can be persevering without being perfect. Perfection and perseverance: these are the two great qualities of concentration: which is to say that it is not enough to know how to concentrate well, it is also necessary to remember that one must do so as often as possible; conversely, it is not enough to remember this, it is also necessary to do so with a maximum of sincerity, hence of efficacy.

13

The fundamental intention of every religion or wisdom is the following: first, discernment between the real and the unreal, and then concentration upon the real. One could also formulate this intention in these terms: truth and way, *prajñā* and *upāya*, doctrine and its corresponding method. One must know that the Absolute or the Infinite—whatever may be the names given it by respective traditions—is what gives meaning to our existence, just as one must know that the essential content of life is the consciousness of this supreme reality, a fact that explains the part to be played by continual prayer; in a word we live to realize the Absolute. To realize the Absolute is to think of it, under one form or another as indicated by revelation and tradition, by a form such as the Japanese *nembutsu* or the Tibetan *Om mani padme hum* or the Hindu *japa-yoga*, not forgetting the Christian and Islamic invocations, such as the Jesus Prayer and the *dhikr* of the dervishes. Here one will find some very different modalities, not only as between one religion and another but also within the fold of each religion, as can be shown, for instance, by the difference between *Jōdo-Shinshū* and Zen. However this may be, it is only on the basis of a genuine spiritual life that we can envisage any kind of external action with a view to defending truth and spirituality in the world.

14

Every religious system comprises within its foundation a characteristic anthropology—both limitative and operative—in the sense that it is founded upon a given aspect of human nature, and that it attributes to this aspect an absolute importance by taking the part for the whole.

Thus for Christianity man is, *de facto*, essentially a sinner, whereas for Islam he is essentially a slave. The results, respectively, are a sacrificial asceticism and a legalistic obedientialism, whose points of departure—necessarily voluntaristic—take no account of man's deiformity, thus of humanity's sufficient reason for being, which cannot be lost.

Now it is this deiformity—by definition intellective—that esoterism properly so called takes as its starting point, and it is upon it that a purely metaphysical tradition such as *Advaita Vedānta* is founded. Metaphysics could not give rise to a voluntaristic, individualistic, moralistic, and sentimental anthropology, which is necessarily bound up with an anthropomorphist theology; rather, it is clearly founded upon that specifically human prerogative that is the intelligence; it could never be contrary to the normal hierarchy of the human faculties and make intelligence depend upon the will, let alone sentiment.

"There is something in the soul that is uncreated and uncreatable, and this is the Intellect": this saying of Eckhart indicates the esoteric transcending of the fragmentary and insufficient anthropology of the exoterisms. Similarly, in Islam there is this Sufic saying: "The Sufi is uncreated."

For the exoterisms, the effects of the "Fall" are quasi-absolute, whence the absolute necessity of the means of grace of a given religion. For esoterism, on the contrary—and strictly speaking there is only one esoterism—the effects of the loss of Paradise could only be relative, otherwise man would cease being man, hence cease being deiform. Now to say that he is deiform—"made in the image of God"—means that in principle he bears within himself the *Logos*, the Revelation, the Redemption, the Sacraments. We say "in principle", for it is all too clear that this virtuality is very seldom actualized, owing to the Fall precisely; whence the necessity, for those who are called to this actualization, of an esoterism that is both doctrinal and methodical, which permits man to re-become himself; to become fully what he is.

15

The world is full of people who complain that they have been seeking but have not found; this is because they have not known how to seek and have only looked for sentimentalities of an individualistic kind. One often hears it said that the priests of such and such a religion are no good or that they have brought religion itself to naught, as if this were possible or as if a man who serves his religion badly did not betray himself exclusively; men quite forget the timeless value of symbols and of the graces they vehicle. The saints have at all times suffered from the inadequacy of certain priests; but far from thinking of rejecting tradition itself for that reason, they have by their own sanctity compensated for whatever was lacking in the contemporary priesthood. The only means of "reforming" a religion is to reform oneself. It is indispensable to grasp the fact that a rite vehicles a far greater value than a personal virtue. A personal initiative that takes on a religious form amounts to nothing in the absence of a traditional framework such as alone can justify that initiative and turn it to advantage, whereas a rite at least will always keep fresh the sap of the whole tradition and hence also its principial efficacy—even if men do not know how to profit thereby.

16

Today two dangers are threatening religion: from the outside, its destruction—be it only as a result of its general desertion—and from the inside, its falsification. The latter, with its pseudo-intellectual pretensions and its fallacious professions of "reform", is immeasurably more harmful than all the "superstition" and "corruption" of which, rightly or wrongly, the representatives of the traditional patrimonies have been accused; this heritage is absolutely irreplaceable, and in the face of it men as such are of no account. Tradition is abandoned, not because people are no longer capable of understanding its language, but because they do not wish to understand it, for this language is made to be understood till the end of the world; tradition is falsified by reducing it to flatness on the plea of making it more acceptable to "our time", as if one could—or should—accommodate truth to error. Admittedly, a need to reply to new questions and new forms of ignorance can always arise. One can and must explain the sacred doctrine, but not at the expense of that which gives it its reason for existing, that is to say, not at the expense of its truth and effectiveness. There could be no question, for instance, of adding to the *Mahāyāna* or of replacing it by a new vehicle, such as would necessarily be of purely human invention; for the *Mahāyāna*—or shall we say Buddhism?—is infinitely sufficient for those who will give themselves the trouble to look higher than their own heads.

It is quite out of the question that a "revelation", in the full sense of the word, should arise in our time, one comparable, that is to say, to the imparting of one of the great *sūtras* or any other primary scripture; the day of revelations is past on this globe and was so already long ago. The inspirations of the saints are of another order, but these could in any case never falsify or invalidate tradition or intrinsic orthodoxy by claiming to improve on it or even to replace it, as some people have suggested. "Our own time" possesses no quality that makes it the measure or the criterion of values in regard to that which is timeless. It is the timeless that, by its very nature, is the measure of our time, as indeed of all other times; and if our time has no place for authentic tradition, then it is self-condemned by that very fact. The Buddha's message, like every other form of the one and only truth, offers itself to every period with an imperishable freshness. It is as true and as urgent in our day as it was two thousand years ago; the fact that mankind finds itself in the "latter days", the days of forgetfulness and decline, only makes that urgency more actual than ever. In fact, there is nothing more urgent, more actual, or more real than metaphysical truth and its demands. It alone can of its own right fill the vacuum left in the contemporary mentality—especially where young people are concerned—by social and political disappointments on the one hand and by the bewildering and indigestible discoveries of modern science on the other. To search for an "ideology" in the hopes of filling up that vacuum—as if it were simply a matter of plugging a hole—is truly a case of "putting the cart before the horse". It is a case of subordinating truth and salvation to narrowly utilitarian and in any case quite external ends, as if the sufficient cause of truth could be found somewhere below truth. The sufficient cause of man is to know the truth, which exists outside and above him; the truth cannot depend for its meaning and existence on the wishes of man. The very word "ideology" shows that truth is not the principal aim people have in mind; to use that word shows that one is scarcely concerned with the difference between true and false and that what one is primarily seeking is a mental deception that will be comfortable and workable, or practicable for purposes of one's own choosing, which is tantamount to abolishing both truth and intelligence.

Outside tradition there can assuredly be found some relative truths or views of partial realities, but outside tradition there does not exist a doctrine that catalyzes absolute truth and transmits liberating notions concerning total reality.

17

The certitude of the Absolute is absolute. The essence of this certitude is that it belongs to our very substance.

Faced with all the possible uncertainties of this world, we must tell ourselves: we have the certitude of the Absolute—of the Sovereign Good—which takes precedence over all other certitudes; with it we possess everything. The best remedy for the malady of doubt is reference to the primal certitude; this certitude which is not only truth, but also salvation.

Given the decadence of mankind, there are men who do not have the supreme certitude; but it may be acquired by faith as well as by reason. It slumbers in the depths of every man; it is the essence of his being and thus constitutes his fundamental vocation.

Say: the certitude of God suffices me; I need not worry over uncertain things. If I have the certitude of God, I will also have the other certitudes that are of use to me. One must not want to know everything or understand everything; on the contrary, one must resign oneself to the uncertainties of the world and of life, given that one possesses the immense treasure that is the certitude of God.

This certitude in principle implies salvation. The certitude of the divine Reality is unconditional; that of salvation is conditional, for it presupposes our total adherence to what is metaphysically certain, which is to say that it depends on the conclusions we draw from our conviction. To be truly conscious of the Sovereign Good is to want to conform to its nature and be united with it, in the measure of our gifts and of grace; possessing intelligence, we *ipso facto* possess will, which is determined by what we know.

The unicity of the known—of the divine Principle—demands the totality of the knower; God is such that we must "love Him with all our faculties"; the known good commits us to love: to union with it. But if the unicity of the object—and God alone is absolutely unique—demands ontologically and logically the totality of the subject, the converse is equally true, *mutatis mutandis*: the totality of the subject aspires to the unicity of the object, in the sense that man, as a central—hence, total—being, is made for knowing the Unique and thus for the certitude of the Absolute. On the one hand, the reality of God determines the nature of man; on the other, the nature of man proves the reality of God.

Certitude of God, peace of heart. O *beata certitudo, O certa beatitudo.*

18

The serenity that transcends cosmic Illusion leads, in principle and altogether logically, to a serenity that transcends the world's and life's accidents. The immanent certitude—in the depths of the heart—of Divine Reality leads, in principle and altogether logically, to all the certitudes we need in the world and life.

Norms and Paradoxes in Initiatic Alchemy

Metaphysical thought essentially presupposes intellection, or let us say intellectual intuition; the latter is not a matter of sentiment, of course, but of pure intelligence. Without this intuition, metaphysical speculation is reduced either to an opaque dogmatism or to a wavering ratiocination; and quite evidently, speculative thought deprived of its intuitive foundation would be unable to prepare the ground for *gnosis*: for direct, concrete, and plenary Knowledge. Let us specify that the possible gaps in the human mind are due, not to fortuitous causes, but to the very conditions of the "dark age", the *kali-yuga*, which has as an effect—among other modes of decadence—a progressive weakening of pure intellection and of the ascending tendencies of the soul; whence the necessity of the religious Revelations, and whence also the problematical phenomenon of gratuitous and divergent philosophies. But man always remains man "made in the image of God"; nothing could prevent, even in these millennia of darkness, the flowering of wisdoms pertaining to the *Sophia Perennis*: such as the *Upanishads*, the *Brahma Sūtras*, and the *Advaita Vedānta*.

The content of the universal and primordial Doctrine is the following, expressed in Vedantic terms: "*Brahman* is Reality; the world is appearance; the soul is not other than *Brahman*." These are the three great theses of integral metaphysics; one positive, one negative, one unitive. Let us specify that in the second affirmation, it is important to understand that "appearance" gives rise to two complementary interpretations: according to the first, the world is illusion, nothingness; according to the second, it is divine Manifestation; the first point of view is upheld by Shankara and Shivaism, and the second by Ramanuja and Vishnuism; approximatively speaking, for there are compensations in both camps. The third of the fundamental affirmations marks as it were the passage from the "Truth" to the "Way", or let us say from the Doctrine to the Method; the soul not being "other than *Brahman*", its vocation is to transcend the world. In other words, since the human intellect has by definition the capacity to conceive and to realize the Absolute, this possibility is its Law; from speculative discernment results operative and unitive concentration. To theology is joined orison; "pray without ceasing".

But there is yet another dimension to be considered, and it is the moral—in certain respects "aesthetic"—climate of spiritual alchemy; this climate basically constitutes what has been called the "initiatic qualification". To the Truth and the Way must be joined Virtue, namely the qualities of humility, charity, justice, and dignity: rigorous knowledge of oneself, benevolent understanding of others, impartial perception of the nature of things, inward and outward participation in the "Motionless Mover"—in the immutable Archetype or the majesty of Being. There is no *sādhana* without *dharma*; no spiritual alchemy without nobleness of character; "Beauty is the splendor of the True."

The point of departure of the Way is the Doctrine, the origin of which is Revelation; man accepts Revelation through intellectual intuition or by that feeling for the True or the Real which is called faith. There is little likelihood of a man being born with knowledge of the integral Doctrine; but it is possible, very exceptionally, that he possess from birth the certitude of the Essential.

Intelligence, by which we comprehend the Doctrine, is either the intellect or reason; reason is the instrument of the intellect. It is through reason that man comprehends the natural phenomena around him and within himself, and it is through it that he is able to describe supernatural things—parallel to the means of expression offered by symbolism—by transposing intuitive knowledge into the order of language. The function of the rational faculty can be to provoke, by means of a given concept, a spiritual intuition; reason is then the flint that makes the spark spring forth. The limit of the Inexpressible varies according to mental structures: what is beyond all expression for some, may be easily expressible for others.

It is all too readily believed that a metaphysical text is a creation of reason because it has the form of a logical demonstration, whereas reason in this case is but the means of transmission. There are mystics who lose interest in a text because it is logical, that is, because they believe it is necessary to transcend this plane; as if logic were a sign of ignorance or illusion, when in fact it is a reflection of universal Causality within our mind.

The desire to transcend the plane of logic is combined, in a certain sectarianism hostile to discursive expression, with the desire to transcend the "scission" between the subject and the object; now this complementary opposition does not prevent the known—whatever the situation of the knower—from being of the loftiest order. The subject and the object are not adversaries; they unite in a fusion that, depending on the content of the perception, can have an interiorizing and liberating virtue, of which aesthetic enjoyment and the union of love are the foremost examples. In *Ātmā*, the triad *Sat, Chit, Ānanda*—"Being, Consciousness, Beatitude"—is not a factor of scission; similarly, the dimensions of physical space do not prevent space from being one, so that we perceive no fissure in it.

What we blame in those who denigrate "metaphysical ratiocination" and the "subject-object opposition" is not so much a given perspective as the exaggeration resulting from it or nourished by it. Excess is in the nature of man; pious exaggeration is finally unavoidable, as is the sectarian mentality. We do not remember who said "all that is excessive is insignificant"; this is quite true, but let us not lose sight of the fact that on the religious plane, hyperbole veils an intention that in the end is merciful; it is then a question of *upāya*, of a "saving stratagem". Doubtless, the voices of wisdom that esoterically either condemn or justify "holy absurdities" may appear "heretical" from the standpoint of a given literalistic orthodoxy, but "God knoweth His own"; the divine Intellect is not limited by a given theology or a given morality. According to the Norm, that which is true saves; according to Grace, that which saves is true.

Unquestionably, the partisans of a symbolist and anti-intellectual intuitionism make a mistake in reproaching speculative intelligence for not being Knowledge as such—which it does not claim to be—and in concluding that it is an obstacle on the Way, whereas, quite evidently, theoretical knowledge is an indispensable stage of the pilgrimage towards total knowledge. Man is a thinking being, and he cannot avoid thought; and "in the beginning was the Word".

—— ·|· ——

There is the perspective of Transcendence and there is the perspective of Immanence; each must be found in the other, as is shown in its own way by the Taoist *Yin-Yang*. There is a subjective Transcendence as there is an objective Immanence: the intellect is transcendent in relation to the individual, as the Creator is immanent in created things.

But here also—in the face of these two mysteries—there are the divergent options of those who make of every complementarity an alternative: some believe that everything has to fall from Heaven; others believe that everything can and must come from our own efforts. Now human intelligence, being theomorphic, possesses in principle a supernatural power; but whatever be the prerogatives of our nature, we can do nothing without God's help: for it is He who causes us to participate in the Knowledge He has of Himself.

In Japanese Buddhism, one distinguishes between "self-power", *jiriki*, and "Other-power", *tariki*; the first refers to Immanence and the second to Transcendence. The first means that everything, in the Way, depends on our own strength and initiative; the second means that everything depends on celestial Grace. In reality, even if one of the viewpoints predominates, both viewpoints have to be combined; for on the one hand, we cannot save ourselves by relying entirely on our own powers, and on the other hand, Heaven will not help us if we, who are created intelligent and free, do not collaborate in our own salvation.

We have seen above that the practice of unitive concentration proceeds from a speculative discernment that justifies and even requires it; now the supports of this concentration are infinitely diverse by reason of the complexity of man, distant reflection of the Infinitude of God.

The modes are not always intelligible at first sight; for example, one might wonder what the relevance is of a discipline such as the Tea Ceremony, which combines ascesis with art, while being materially based on manipulations that seem *a priori* insignificant, but are ennobled by their sacralization. First of all, one must take into account the fact that in the Far Easterner sensorial intuition is more developed than the speculative gift; also, that the practical sense and the aesthetic sense, as well as the taste for symbolism are at the basis of his spiritual temperament. In the Tea Ceremony, the symbolic and morally correct act—the "profound" Act, if one will—is meant to bring about a sort of Platonic *anamnesis* or a unitive consciousness; whereas with the white man of the East and the West it is the Idea that is supposed to lead to correct and virtuous acts. The man of the yellow race goes from sensorial experience to intellection, roughly speaking, whereas with the white man, it is more or less the converse that takes place: in starting out from concepts, or from habitual mental images, he understands and classifies phenomena without, however, feeling the need to consciously integrate them into his spiritual life; except incidentally or when it is a question of traditionally accepted symbols.

Men are different: some like to express themselves by subtle allusions, for fear of limiting the real, whereas others prefer direct and analytical expression, for fear of remaining imprecise—it takes all kinds to make a world—but all the possibilities can be combined, man not being a closed system. Besides, one cannot help defining things, but care must be taken not to limit them too much in defining them; and if discursive expression is a double-edged sword, it is because reality presents a thousand facets.

The Tea Ceremony signifies that we ought to perform all the activities and manipulations of daily life according to primordial perfection, which is pure symbolism, pure consciousness of the Essential, perfect beauty, and self-domination. The intention is basically the same in the craft initiations of the West—including Islam—but the formal foundation is then the production of useful objects and not the symbolism of gestures; this being so, the stone mason intends, parallel to his work, to hew and fashion his soul in view of union with God. And thus there is to be found in all the crafts and all the arts a spiritual model that, in the Muslim world, often refers to one of the prophets mentioned in the Koran; any professional or homemaking activity is a kind of revelation. As for the adherents of Zen, they readily seek their inspiration in "ordinary life", not because it is trivial, to be sure, but because—inasmuch as it is woven of symbolisms—it mysteriously implies the "Buddha nature".

All this evokes the question of the Symbol and of symbolism; what is the role of the Symbol in the economy of spiritual life? We have shown that the object of concentration is not necessarily an Idea, but that it can also be a symbolic sign, a sound, an image, or an activity: the monosyllable *Om*, mystical diagrams—*mandalas*—and images of the Divinities are in their way vehicles of consciousness of the Absolute, without the intervention of a doctrinal element; the "contemplation of the naked Lady", in certain circles of the troubadours or the *Fedeli d'Amore*, suggests a vision of the Infinite and of pure Being—not a seduction, but a catharsis. The pre-eminence either of the Idea or of the Symbol is a question of opportuneness rather than of principle; by the nature of things, the modes of the Way are as diverse as men are, and as complex as the human soul. But whatever be our points of departure—Idea or Symbol or their combination— there is also, and essentially, concentration on the Void, concentration made of certitude and serenity; as Shankara said: "That which is the cessation of mental agitation and the supreme peacefulness, . . . that is the true Benares, and it is that which I am."

For a certain mysticism met with in all traditional climates, only sentiment, not intelligence, offers the solution to the main problem of our existence, namely the meaning of life; eschatology then takes on the function of metaphysics. In this promotion of feeling, the word "truth" is still used, but it means that which liberates us while granting us a happiness which we experience as being fundamental and lasting; truth is then no longer a principle comprising the most diverse contents, it is simply a given content dogmatized; it is forgotten that the true is the nature of things, and that nothing can take precedence over this in the vision of the real. Still within this mental and moral climate, intelligence—presented as "analytical" and "separative"—is opposed to sentiment viewed according to its synthetic and unitive aspect; and what is constructed is a deformed image of man, as if he were the victim of a deceptive intelligence, and liberated by sentimental solutions.

This is not to say that sentiment could not, for its part, be a mode of knowledge as well, for to love something worthy of being loved is to "know" it in a certain way; but this is no reason for believing that sentiment, because of its spontaneous, unarticulated, and quasi-magical character, is the only mode of knowledge possible, or the loftiest mode. A fact that seems to justify the sentimental intuitionists in question, but the real bearing of which they hardly suspect, is the following, and it is incontestable: a phenomenon of beauty can be more suddenly and more profoundly convincing than a logical explanation, whence this maxim: "The Buddhas save not by their preaching alone, but also by their superhuman beauty." Thus, the Platonic opinion that "Beauty is the splendor of the True" expresses unequivocally the profound, intimate, ontological relationship between the Real and the Beautiful, or between Being and Harmony; a relationship that implies—as we have just said—that Beauty is sometimes a more striking and transforming argument than a discursive proof; not logically more adequate, but humanly more miraculous.

To speak of Beauty is to speak of Love; and it is known how important this idea of Love is in all religions and all spiritual alchemies. The reason for this is that Love is the tendency towards Union: this tendency can be a movement, either towards the Immutable, the Absolute, or towards the Limitless, the Infinite. On the plane of human relations, a particular love is the support for Love as such; and the love of man for woman can be compared to the liberating tendency towards the divine Infinitude—woman personifying All-Possibility—whereas the love of woman for man is comparable to the stabilizing tendency towards the divine Center, which offers all certitude and all security; however, each partner participates in the other's position, given that each is a human being and that in this respect the sexual division is secondary. As for sexuality in itself, the Sufi Ibn Arabi deems sexual union to be, in the natural order, the most adequate image of supreme Knowledge: of the Extinction in *Allāh* of the "Knower through *Allāh*".

The initiatic journey comprises an Enlightenment that is produced either gradually, or at one single time, or at the moment of death, when the psychosomatic drama favors this irruption of Light. It is, at one degree or another, *Moksha, Bodhi, Satori*; ecstasy is an analogous mode, but of a different order, for of itself it does not produce a lasting station. Enlightenment—which moreover presupposes persevering efforts and quite often severe trials—has often been presented as a mystery of Love, precisely because it is a question of an integral and quasi-existential reality that transcends the mental play of conjectures and conclusions; *l'Amor che muove il sole e l'altre stelle*.

The initiatic journey presents two moral dimensions of primary importance, one exclusive and ascetical and the other inclusive and symbolist, or aesthetic if one may say so. Among aspirants to Liberation, there are first of all those who, in the name of Truth, withdraw from the world, such as monks or *sannyāsins*; then there are those who, in the name of the same Truth, remain in the world and seek to transmute into gold the lead the world offers *a priori*, such as the adepts of the knightly and craft initiations. If Shankara recommended the ascetical path, that is because it is the surest, given human weakness; but he specified in one of his writings that the "one delivered in this life", the *jīvan mukta*, can adapt himself harmoniously and victoriously to any social situation conforming to universal *Dharma*, as is shown at the highest level by the example of Krishna. On the one hand, one must see God in Himself, beyond the world, in the Emptiness of Transcendence; on the other hand and *ipso facto*, one must see God everywhere: first of all in the miraculous existence of things and then in their positive and theomorphic qualities; once Transcendence is understood, Immanence reveals itself of itself.

In the Buddhist as well as the Hindu climate, one encounters a mystical altruism that protests against "seeking a selfish salvation": apparently, one should not wish to save oneself, one should at the same time wish to save others, or even everyone, at least by intention. Now a selfish salvation is a contradiction in terms; an egoist does not obtain salvation, there is no place in Heaven for a miser. Altruists do not see that in the Way, the distinction between "I" and "others" disappears: any salvific realization is so to speak realization as such, and this being so, a realization obtained by a given person always has an invisible radiance that blesses the ambience. There is no need for a sentimentalism that intends to come to the rescue of Truth; for with the True, Love is already a given, the circle closes with a transpersonal and infinitely generous Beatitude. Love of the Creator implies Love of creatures; and true charity implies Love of God—of divine Reality, whatever be its Name.

The Advaitic doctrine comprises the crucial idea of hierarchized Truth: first of all there is the one and absolute Truth, but this latter does not exclude the diverse and relative truths; on the contrary, it supports them, since they offer to common mortals all that they are able to understand and all that can save them. On the one hand, what is true saves *ipso facto*; on the other hand, that is true which possesses a saving power.

This is what must not be lost sight of when considering the perplexing diversity of liberating Ways—not just any sects, but the intrinsically orthodox Ways, whatever the demerits of the men who represent them. Doubtless there are demanding doctrines that cannot satisfy every kind of understanding; but there are truths all men must acknowledge, actions all must perform, beauties all must realize; which is to say that there is a Message for the least of mortals. Truth, Prayer, and Virtue; everything is there.

EDITOR'S NOTES

Numbers in bold indicate pages in the text for which the following citations and explanations are provided.

Prerogatives of the Human State

1: The *"Fall"* refers to the eating of the forbidden fruit by Adam and Eve in the Garden of Eden, the "original sin" (cf. Gen. 2-3, *Sūrah* "The Heights" [7]:19-26), and their subsequent banishment from the earthly Paradise.

"God is beautiful and He loves Beauty" (*hadīth*).

2: Note 1: The *Kabbalah* is a mystical stream of esoteric teachings within the Judaic tradition.

The *Koran*, the holy book of Islam, comprises a series of revelations made to the prophet Muhammad (570-632).

The *Vedānta* is the non-dualistic school of Hindu philosophy, based on the teachings of the *Upanishads*, which are regarded as the synthesis and culmination of the Vedic teachings.

3: "Behold, the kingdom of God is *within you*" (Luke 17:21).

4: Note 4: All four canonical Christian gospels recount the occasion on which *Jesus treated the temple merchants harshly*, overturning the tables of the money changers who had turned the sacred precinct into a "den of robbers" (Matt. 21:12-17; Mark 11:15-19; Luke 19:45-48; John 2:13-16).

5: Note 5: *"Iron Age"*: According to the traditional Hindu doctrine of cycles time is qualitatively divided into *mahāyuga*s or "great ages", each of which comprises four lesser ages (*yuga*s) or periods of time, of which the *Kali-Yuga* ("iron" or "dark") is the last; it "marks the end of a great cyclic period of terrestrial humanity" (Frithjof Schuon, *The Transcendent Unity of Religions* [Wheaton, IL: Theosophical Publishing House, 1993], p. xxxiii). This doctrine is not exclusive to the Hinduism but it is there given its fullest expression.

7: The Vedantic affirmations "Brahman *is Reality*", "*the world is merely appearance*", and "*the soul is not different from* Brahman" are traditionally ascribed to Shankara (788-820), the foremost exponent of *Advaita Vedānta*, whom the author considered to be the greatest of all Hindu metaphysicians. For a fuller explication of this doctrine of non-dualism (*advaita*), see the author's "*Vedānta*", in *Spiritual Perspectives and Human Facts: A New Translation with Selected Letters*, ed. James S. Cutsinger (Bloomington, Indiana: World Wisdom, 2007), pp. 97-129, "Tracing *Māyā*", in *Light on the Ancient Worlds: A New Translation with Selected Letters*, ed. Deborah Casey (Bloomington, Indiana: World Wisdom, 2007), pp. 75-82, and "*Ātmā-Māyā*", in *Form and Substance in the Religions* (Bloomington, Indiana: World Wisdom, 2002), pp. 31-41.

On the Islamic formulations that "*God alone is*", "*there is no other divinity*", and "*Muhammad is the Messenger of God*", see the author's commentary on the *Shahādah*, the fundamental "testimony" or profession of faith in Islam, in *Understanding Islam: A New Translation with Selected Letters*, ed. Patrick Laude (Bloomington, Indiana: World Wisdom, 2007).

"*It is not for the love of the spouse that the spouse is dear, but for the love of* Ātmā *which is in him*" (*Brihadāranyaka Upanishad*, 2.4.5).

7-8: The German Dominican, Meister Eckhart (1260-1327), whom the author regarded as the greatest of Christian metaphysicians and esoterists, made a distinction *in divinis* between the "Godhead" (*Gottheit*) or *transpersonal Divinity*, and *Gott* ("God") or personal Divinity. Eckhart also proclaimed that "There is something in the soul that is *uncreated* and uncreatable" (*aliquid est in anima quod est increatum et increabile*), namely the pure *Intellect*.

9: "*Goodness—and along with it beatitude—is the splendor of the true*" is a variation on the axiom "Beauty is the splendor of the true", attributed by the author to Plato (427-347 B.C.), the greatest of the ancient Greek philosophers.

12: *Bernard* of Clairvaux (1090-1153) was a Cistercian monk and author of numerous homilies on the *Song of Songs*.

The Latin "O *beata certitudo, o certa beatitudo*" ("O blessed certitude, O certain beatitude") is the author's variation on Bernard's "O *beata solitudo, o sola beatitudo*" ("O blessed solitude, O sole beatitude").

Man in the Cosmogonic Projection

15: The keystone of *transformist evolution* is the ill-founded Darwinian notion of the transformation of species. As the author has observed elsewhere, "Transformist evolutionism offers a patent example of 'horizontality' in the domain of the natural sciences, owing to the fact that it puts a biological evolution of 'ascending' degrees in place of a cosmogonic emanation of 'descending' degrees" (*Roots of the Human Condition* [Bloomington, Indiana: World Wisdom, 1991], p. 5).

17: *Krishna* is the eighth *avatāra* of the Hindu god Vishnu, the second in the Hindu triad (*trimūrti*), Brahmā being the first and Shiva the third. Hindu tradition tells of Krishna's youthful dalliance with the adoring *gopīs*, or cowherd girls, of Vrindavan.

18: *Man being* imago Dei: "So God created man in his own image, in the image of God created he him; male and female created he them" (Gen. 1:27).

19: *Lalla Yogishwari* was a fourteenth century Kashmiri poet and saint. Among the gems of her poetry, from which the author is quoting, are the lines: "My guru spake to me but one precept. He said unto me, 'From without enter thou the inmost part.' That to me became a rule and a precept, *and that is why, naked, I dance.*"

The author says elsewhere concerning the Semitic doctrine of *creatio ex nihilo* ("creation out of nothing"): "When one speaks traditionally of *creatio ex nihilo*, what is meant, on the one hand, is that creatures do not derive from a pre-existing matter and, on the other, that the 'incarnation' of possibilities cannot in any way affect the immutable Plenitude of the Principle" (Frithjof Schuon, *From the Divine to the Human: A New Translation with Selected Letters*, ed. Patrick Laude [Bloomington, Indiana: World Wisdom, 2007], p. 14).

Note 5: "Brahman *is reality; the world is appearance*" is a Vedantic saying traditionally attributed to Shankara (see editor's note for "Prerogatives of the Human State", p. 7).

22: The words of an ancient liturgical hymn for Holy Saturday—"O truly necessary sin of Adam, which by the death of Christ is done away! O happy fault (*felix culpa*), which merited such and so great a Redeemer!"—are traditionally ascribed to Augustine (354-430), Bishop of the North African city of Hippo, and the greatest of the Western Church Fathers.

"*And God saw that it was good*": "And God saw every thing that he had made, and, behold, it was very good" (Gen. 1:31).

The Pali phrase, *Sabbe sattā sukhi hontu*, or "*May all beings be happy*", is chanted as a *mantra* in Buddhism.

22: Note 10: "*Inasmuch as ye have done it unto one of the least of these my* *brethren, ye have done it unto Me*" (Matt. 25:40; cf. Matt. 25:45).

Note 11: The Church Father *Irenaeus* (c. 130-c. 200) taught that "the Son of God became the Son of man so that man, by entering into communion with the Word and thus receiving divine sonship, might become a son of God" (*Against Heresies*, 3:19).

The doctrine of *apocatastasis*, or universal salvation, was expounded by Origen (185-252); in its esoteric dimension the doctrine links universal salvation to the recovery, through sleepless attention, of man's primordial unity in God.

The Play of Masks

23: *The Eckhartian* distinguo refers to Meister Eckhart's (see editor's note for "Prerogatives of the Human State", pp. 7-8) distinction *between the "inner man" and the "outer man"*.

"*True man and true God*": the doctrine of the "two natures" of Christ was ratified at the Council of Chalcedon in 451 and is a foundation-stone of Christian theology.

"*Laugh with those who laugh and weep with those who weep*" (Rom. 12:15).

Note 1: For *the play of Krishna* see editor's note for "Man in the Cosmogonic Projection", p. 17. In the *Bhagavad Gītā* Krishna reveals himself in all his splendor to the charioteer *Arjuna*.

Note 2: William *Shakespeare* (1564-1616) was a playwright, poet, and actor, and is widely regarded as the greatest writer in the English language. *Hamlet* is one of his tragedies.

Augustus (63 B.C.-14 A.D.) was the first Roman *Emperor*, ruling from 27 B.C.-14 A.D.

25: The *wedding at Cana*, where Christ consecrated or blessed marriage and changed the water into wine, is recounted in John 2:1-11. It is *Mary* who says to Jesus that the guests "*have no wine*" (John 2:3).

Note 4: *Diogenes* of Sinope (c. 412-323 B.C.) was a Greek cynic philosopher.

Omar Khayyam (1048-1125) was a Persian astronomer, mathematician, and poet, whose *Rubaiyat* ("quatrains") conceal a mystical apprehension of God under a veil of seeming skepticism and hedonism.

Till Eulenspiegel was a medieval German trickster and fool, whose pranks were designed to expose human vices; *Nasruddin Khoja* is *mutatis mutandis* his Turkish equivalent.

The *heyoka* is the trickster figure in the mythology of the North American Plains Indians. For some remarks on the subject see the author's *The Feathered Sun: Plains Indians in Art and Philosophy* (Bloomington, Indiana: World Wisdom, 1990), pp. 88-89.

Note 5: For *Meister Eckhart* see editor's note for "Prerogatives of the Human State", p. 7.

Abu al-Qasim *Al-Junayd* (830-910) was a Sufi mystic of Persian extraction who taught in Baghdad.

26: The *Song of Songs* (or "Song of Solomon"), a book of the Hebrew Bible, is an allegorical love poem, traditionally interpreted by Jews and Christians to signify the mystical relationship between God and the soul.

The *Gītā Govinda* ("Song of Govinda"), written by the Sanskrit poet Jayadeva (b.c. 1200), is a twelfth century work concerning the love of Krishna, an *avatāra* or incarnation of Vishnu, for his consort Radha.

"*Thou art all fair, my love, there is no spot in thee*" (Song of Sol. 4:7).

27: Note 8: The *Blessed Virgin* is Mary, Mother of Jesus. For a fuller discussion of Mary as Virgin and Mother, see the author's "Christic and Virginal Mysteries", in *Gnosis: Divine Wisdom: A New Translation with Selected Letters*, ed. James S. Cutsinger (Bloomington, Indiana: World Wisdom, 2006), pp. 119-124.

The apostle *Luke* was one of the four evangelists, or ascribed authors of the canonical Gospels, as well as the author of the Acts of the Apostles in the New Testament.

Jalal ad-Din Rumi (1207-73) was one of the greatest Sufi mystics and poets, and the founder of the Mevlevi order.

28: "*The righteous man sins seven times a day*" (Prov. 24:16).

"*Why callest thou me good? There is none good but one, that is, God*" (Mark 10:18; Luke 18:19).

Note 9: Johann Wolfgang von *Goethe* (1749-1832) was a German poet, novelist, and playwright. In his work *Faust*, published in two parts, in 1808 and posthumously in 1832, he reworked the German legend about the scholar who sells his soul to Mephistopheles (the *devil*) in exchange for boundless knowledge and power. The author has written elsewhere that Goethe "was the victim of his epoch owing to the fact that humanism in general and Kantianism in particular had impaired his tendency toward a vast and finely shaded wisdom; he thus became, quite paradoxically, the spokesman of a perfectly bourgeois 'horizontality'. . . . All the same, there is unquestionably great scope in the human substance of Goethe: a scope manifested by the at once lofty and generous quality of his mind" (*To Have a Center: A New Translation with Selected Letters*, ed. Harry Oldmeadow [Bloomington, Indiana: World Wisdom, 2015], p. 13).

David (c. 1040-970 B.C.) was the second king of Israel and Judah, the composer of the Psalms, and, according to Christian tradition, an ancestor of Jesus Christ. For further commentary on David by the author, see "David, Honen, Shankara", in *To Have a Center: A New Translation with Selected Letters*, ed. Harry Oldmeadow (Bloomington, Indiana: World Wisdom, 2015), pp. 105-112.

"Mine iniquities . . . are more than the hairs of mine head" (Psalm 40:12).

30: The chapter *"Eschatologie universelle"* in the author's *Sur les traces de la Religion pérenne* (Paris: Le Courrier du Livre, 1982) appears in English as "Universal Eschatology" in *Survey of Metaphysics and Esoterism* (Bloomington, Indiana: World Wisdom, 1985, 2000), pp. 77-88.

Ex Nihilo, In Deo

31: For *creatio ex nihilo* see editor's note for "Man in the Cosmogonic Projection", p. 19.

Note 1: *God fashioned Adam "of earth"*: "And the Lord God formed man of the dust of the ground, and breathed into his nostrils the breath of life; and man became a living soul" (Gen 2:7).

32: *Vincit omnia Veritas*—Latin for "truth conquers all"—is a traditional maxim, often quoted by the author, based upon the words of 1 Esdras 3:12: *super omnia autem vincit veritas*, "But truth conquereth over all" (cf. 1 Esdras 4:35, 41).

33: *"Our Father who art in heaven, Hallowed be Thy Name. Thy kingdom come"* (Matt. 6:9-10; Luke 11:2-3). For the author's commentary on the Lord's Prayer see *To Have a Center: A New Translation with Selected Letters*, ed. Harry Oldmeadow, pp. 97-103.

The Church Father Athanasius (c. 296-373) articulated the *patristic formula* that "The Son of *God became man that man might become God*" (*Incarnation*, 54:3); see also editor's note for "Man in the Cosmogonic Projection", p. 22, Note 11.

34: The "*motionless mover*", or Unmoved Mover, is the classic expression of the ancient Greek philosopher *Aristotle* (384-322 B.C.), for the divine Principle, as in *Metaphysics*, 1072b.

"*Made in the image of God*": "And God said, Let us make man in our image, after our likeness" (Gen. 1:26).

For *the gopīs dancing around Krishna* see editor's note for "Man in the Cosmogonic Projection", p. 17.

The *Kaaba* (literally "cube") is the most sacred sanctuary of Islam, dating back to the patriarch Abraham, who was instructed by God to build it nearby the miraculous well of Zamzam in the valley of Mecca (see *Sūrah* "Pilgrimage" [22]:26-27). The cube-like structure is the point of orientation for the daily prayers and is ritually circumambulated during the pilgrimage.

The *Sun Dance* is one of the principal rituals of the American Plains Indians. See the author's "The Sun Dance", in *The Feathered Sun: Plains Indians in Art and Philosophy*, pp. 90-100.

Note 3: The prophet *Abraham* is a patriarchal figure in the monotheistic traditions of Judaism, Christianity, and Islam, and is considered the father of both the Jews and the Arabs through his sons Isaac and Ishmael.

In the Face of Contingency

37: Note 1: *Hamlet's drama* is presented in the tragedy *Hamlet* by William Shakespeare (see editor's note for "The Play of Masks", p. 23, Note 2).

For *Aristotle* see editor's note for "*Ex Nihilo, in Deo*", p. 34.

38: "*Beauty is the splendor of the true*" is an axiom attributed by the author to Plato.

40: *Pyrrhonism* is the skeptical philosophy of the ancient Greek, Pyrrho of Elis (c. 360-270 B.C.).

Note 3: Albert *Einstein* (1879-1955) was a German physicist and mathematician who developed the general theory of relativity.

Ptolemean astronomy was based on geocentric models developed by the ancient astronomer Ptolemaeus, or Ptolemy (c. 90-c. 168). These astronomical models remained authoritative until the time of the scientific revolution of the seventeenth century.

43: The saying of *Meister Eckhart* (see editor's note for "Prerogatives of the Human State", p. 7), "*The more he blasphemeth, the more he praiseth God*" is one of the twenty-eight articles condemned by the papal bull *In agro dominico* in 1329.

René *Descartes* (1596-1650) propounded a philosophical method based upon the systematic doubting of everything except one's own self-consciousness, as summed up in the Latin phrase *cogito ergo sum* ("*I think, therefore I am*").

Thomas Aquinas (c. 1225-74) was an immensely influential Italian Dominican priest and scholastic theologian, known in Catholic tradition as the "Angelic Doctor". His best-known works are the *Summa theologiae* and the *Summa Contra Gentiles*.

44: "Behold, *the kingdom of God is within you*" (Luke 17:21).

Note 9: For further commentary on *Eve* see the author's "The Primordial Tree", in *Esoterism as Principle and as Way: A New Translation with Selected Letters*, ed. Harry Oldmeadow (Bloomington, Indiana: World Wisdom, 2007), pp. 71-82; on *Mary* see the author's "Christic and Virginal Mysteries", in *Gnosis: Divine Wisdom; A New Translation with Selected Letters*, ed. James S. Cutsinger, pp. 119-124.

Delineations of Original Sin

47: Note 1: The *Immaculate Conception* is the Roman Catholic dogma that, from the first moment of her conception, Mary was free from all stain of original sin.

48: "Behold, *the kingdom of God is within you*" (Luke 17:21).

"Thou shalt love the Lord thy God *with all thy heart, and with all thy soul, and with all thy strength, and with all thy mind*" (Luke 10:27); "this is the first and great commandment," says Christ (Matt. 22:37; *cf.* Mark 12:30, Deut. 6:5).

The Apocalypse is also known as the Book of Revelation, the last book in the New Testament, and is traditionally attributed to the evangelist John.

"So then because thou art lukewarm, and neither cold nor hot, I will spew thee out of my mouth" (Rev. 3:16).

For the teaching "Brahman *is real; the world is illusory; the soul is not other than* Brahman", see editor's note for "Prerogatives of the Human State", p. 7.

Note 2: For *Shankara* see editor's note for "Prerogatives of the Human State", p. 7.

Note 3: According to the Apostle James, he who knows to do good and does not do it, commits a sin: "Therefore to him that knoweth to do good, and doeth it not, to him it is sin" (James 4:17).

49: *The drama of the forbidden fruit*, describing the Fall of Adam and Eve in the Garden of Eden, is recounted in Genesis 2-3.

"After this manner therefore pray ye: *Our Father who art in heaven*, hallowed be thy name" (Matt. 6:9; *cf.* Luke 11:2).

50: The building of the *Tower of Babel* and the confounding of human language are told of in Genesis 11:4-9.

The *Titans* were the oldest race of Greek gods, who, under the leadership of Cronus, resisted the power of Zeus and the other Olympians; *Prometheus* stole fire from the Olympian gods; Daedalus fashioned wings for himself and his son, *Icarus*, but the young boy flew too close to the sun, melting the wax in the wings and plunging him to his death.

The *forbidden tree* afforded "knowledge of *good* and *evil*" (Gen. 2:17).

According to the Koran, God, having "taught Adam all the names" of the *creatures*, commanded him, "O Adam! Inform them of *their names*", and the *angels* were in turn commanded, "*Prostrate* yourselves before Adam" (*Sūrah* "The Cow" [2]:31, 33, 34).

"And *Enoch* walked with God, and he was not, for God took him" (Gen. 5:24; cf. Heb. 11:5).

The *patriarch Enoch* (Idris in Islam), son of Seth and the great grandson of Adam, was taken directly to Heaven by God: "And *Enoch* walked with God, and he was not, for God took him" (Gen. 5:24; cf. Heb. 11:5).

Note 6: The teaching of *Meister Eckhart* (see editor's note for "Prerogatives of the Human State", p. 7) that *"there is something in the soul* [anima] *which is uncreated and uncreatable;* if the whole soul were such, it would be uncreated and uncreatable, *and this is the Intellect* [Intellectus]" was among the articles for which he was charged with heresy, and which he himself subsequently revoked "insofar as they could generate in the minds of the faithful a heretical opinion" (The Bull *In agro dominico* [1329]).

On Intention

51: Note 1: Blaise *Pascal* (1623-62) was a French mathematician, physicist, and Christian philosopher. His critique of what he saw as the casuistry of *the Jesuits* appeared in *Les Provinciales* ("The Provincial Letters") in 1656-57.

52: "*There is no right superior to that of the truth*" is a traditional Hindu maxim attributed to the Maharajahs of Benares.

"*Ye shall know them by their fruits.* Do men gather grapes of thorns, or figs of thistles? Even so every good tree bringeth forth good fruit; but a corrupt tree bringeth forth evil fruit" (Matt. 7:16-17).

Note 2: *Fra Angelico* (1387-1455) was a Dominican friar of the monastery of Fiesole, Italy, and a famous painter of the Florentine School.

54: The injunction "*Know thyself*" is carved into the lintel of Apollo's Temple at Delphi.

The *good thief* was one of two unnamed criminals who were crucified with Jesus. After rebuking the other thief for saying to Jesus, "If thou be Christ, save thyself and us", the *good thief* said, "Lord, remember me when thou comest into thy kingdom." Jesus replied to him, "Verily I say unto thee, Today shalt thou be with me in *Paradise*" (Luke 23:39-43).

Augustine (354-430), the Bishop of the North African city of Hippo and one of the greatest of the Western Church Fathers, was the author of *The City of God* and *Confessions*.

Regnum Dei intra vos est is Latin for "The kingdom of God is within you" (Luke 17:21).

56: "*For the love of God*": "Thou shalt *love* the Lord thy *God* with all thy heart, and with all thy soul, and with all thy strength, and with all thy mind" (Luke 10:27; cf. Matt. 22:37, Mark 12:30, Deut. 6:5).

"With what measure ye mete, it shall be measured to you again" (Matt. 7:2).

"Vox populi, vox Dei" is Latin for "The voice of the people is the voice of God."

Note 7: *John of the Cross* (1542-91) was a Spanish priest and mystic, and co-founder, with Teresa of Avila, of the reformed or Discalced Carmelites.

Note 8: "Give not that which is holy unto the dogs, *neither cast ye your pearls before swine*, lest they trample them under their feet, and turn again and rend you" (Matt. 7:6).

57: *"Made in the image of God"*: "And God said, Let us make man in our image, after our likeness" (Gen. 1:26).

58: For *David* see editor's note for "The Play of Masks", p. 28, Note 9.

Remarks on Charity

59: *"Let not thy left hand know what thy right hand doeth"* (Matt. 6:3).

No Initiative without Truth

61: René *Guénon* (1886-1951), a French metaphysician and prolific scholar of religions, was one of the formative authorities of the perennialist school, and a frequent contributor to the journal *Études Traditionnelles*. His work *Orient et Occident* (1924) ("East and West") was the first to elaborate a comprehensive critique of the modern West, later more fully developed in *La Crise du Monde Moderne* (1927) ("The Crisis of the Modern World") and *Le Règne de la Quantité et les Signes des Temps* (1945) ("The Reign of Quantity and the Signs of the Times").

Ananda K. *Coomaraswamy* (1877-1947), for many years curator of Indian art in the Boston Museum of Fine Arts, was one of the founding figures of the perennialist school and the prolific author of numerous books and articles on art, religion, and metaphysics.

A *categorical imperative* refers to an absolute or unconditional requirement. The phrase is most commonly associated with the German philosopher, Immanuel Kant (1724-1804) and his *Groundwork for the Metaphysics of Morals* (1785).

63: *Spinozist humanism* refers to the work of Jewish philosopher Baruch Spinoza (1632-77), who construed the existence of the Divine in such a way as to equate its reality with that of nature, God being the universal substance of which all things are made.

Deist humanism refers to the eighteenth-century philosophy of deism which, basing itself on the evidence of nature, accepted the existence of a creator God, but rejected Revelation, authority, and institutional religion.

Kantian humanism describes the work of Immanuel *Kant* (1724-1804), a German philosopher influenced by Enlightenment thinkers such as Rousseau. Kant insisted that man's knowledge is limited to the domain of sensible objects and that the idea of God is no more than a postulate of reason having no objective certainty.

Freemasonic humanism refers not to the medieval guilds of stone masons, but to the popular eighteenth century movement that sought to undermine and eradicate the authority of the monarchy and the Church.

Marxism is a political ideology deriving from the work of Karl Marx (1818-1883), who developed a philosophy of dialectical materialism. One of his most famous formulations was "*Religion* is the *opium* of *the people*".

64: *Lao Tzu* (sixth century B.C.) was the founder of Taoism and author of the *Tao Te Ching*, which states that "*When the inferior man hears about the* Tao*, he laughs at it; it would not be the* Tao *if he did not laugh at it. . . . The self-evidence of the* Tao *is taken for darkness*" (chap. 41).

Swami *Vivekananda* (1863-1902), a disciple of Ramakrishna, was greatly influenced by the ideas of such modern Western social theorists as John Stuart Mill, which led to his joining the *Brahmo Samāj*, a nineteenth century Hindu reform movement. For the author's more extended commentary on Vivekananda and his relationship to Ramakrishna see "*Vedānta*", in *Spiritual Perspectives and Human Facts: A New Translation with Selected Letters*, ed. James S. Cutsinger, pp. 125-26.

The *Bhagavad Gītā* is one of the principal scriptures of the Hindu tradition and a part of the epic *Mahābhārata*.

65: For the "dark" or "*iron age*" see editor's note for "Prerogatives of the Human State", p. 5, Note 3.

Being Conscious of the Real

67: The Latin phrase *credo ut intelligam* ("I believe so that I may understand") is associated with *Anselm* (c. 1033-1109), Archbishop of Canterbury and one of the most important of the medieval scholastics, who prefaced his *ontological argument* for the existence of God with the words: "I do not seek to understand so that I may believe; but I believe so that I may understand".

"Blessed are they that have not seen, and yet have believed" (John 20:29).

The human heart is either "liquid" or "hardened": "He hath blinded their eyes, and hardened their heart; that they should not see with their eyes, nor understand with their heart, and be converted, and I should heal them" (John 12:40; cf. Exod. 7:13, Deut. 2:30, 2 Chron. 36:13, Isa. 63:17, *passim*).

The human heart . . . has also been compared to a mirror that is either polished or rusted: "There is a means of polishing all things whereby rust may be removed; that which polishes the heart is the remembrance of God" (*hadīth*).

68: *The parable of the persistent widow and the unjust judge* is found in Luke 18:1-8.

Paul (c. 5-c. 67), formerly Saul of Tarsus before his conversion on the road to Damascus (see Acts 9:1-22), was the Apostle to whom are attributed fourteen of the twenty-seven books of the New Testament. In his letter to the Thessalonians he wrote: "Rejoice always, *pray without ceasing*, give thanks in all circumstances; for this is the will of God in Christ Jesus for you" (1 Thess. 5:16-18).

"And he (Jesus) said unto another, *Follow me*. But he said, Lord, suffer me first to go and bury my father. Jesus said unto him, *Let the dead bury their dead*: but go thou and preach *the kingdom of God*" (Luke 9:59-60; Matt. 8:22).

"The *kingdom of God is within you*" (Luke 17:21).

For "*Brahman is real*" see author's note for "Prerogatives of the Human State", p. 7.

Note 1: "*But thou, when thou prayest, enter into thy closet, and when thou hast shut thy door, pray to thy Father which is in secret; and thy Father which seeth in secret shall reward thee openly*" (Matt. 6:6).

"And Jesus said unto him, *No man, having put his hand to the plough, and looking back, is fit for the kingdom of God*" (Luke 9:62).

69: *Christ prescribed loving one's enemies and turning the other cheek*: "But love ye your enemies, and do good, and lend, hoping for nothing in return; and your reward shall be great, and ye shall be sons of the Highest, for he is kind to the unthankful and to the evil" (Luke 6.35); and "And unto him who smiteth thee on the one cheek offer also the other; and him that taketh away thy cloak forbid not to take they coat also" (Luke 6:29).

"Beauty is the splendor of the true" is an axiom attributed by the author to Plato.

"Thou shalt *love* the Lord thy *God with all thy heart, and with all thy soul, and with all thy strength, and with all thy mind*" (Luke 10:27); "this is the first and great commandment," says Christ (Matt. 22:37; *cf.* Mark 12:30, Deut. 6:5).

The Liberating Passage

72: For a more detailed explication of *"the human body . . . is a symbol-sacrament"* see the author's "The Message of the Human Body", in *From the Divine to the Human: A New Translation with Selected Letters*, ed. Patrick Laude, pp. 75-86.

"Made in the image of God": "So God created man in his own image, in the image of God created he him; male and female created he them" (Gen. 1:27).

73: For *Plato* see editor's note for "Prerogatives of the Human State", p. 9.

Appendix

Selections from Letters and Other Previously Unpublished Writings

77: Selection 1: "The Book of Keys", No. 1091, "Truth, Salvation, Beauty".

Selection 2: Unpublished article, "On Love", c. 1945.

78: *"In the image of God"*: "So God created man in his own image, in the image of God created he him; male and female created he them" (Gen. 1:27).

Muhyi al-Din Ibn Arabi (1165-1240), author of numerous works including *Meccan Revelations* and *Bezels of Wisdom*, was a prolific and profoundly influential Sufi mystic, known in tradition as the *Shaykh al-Akbar*, that is, the "great master".

Selection 3: "The Book of Keys", No. 1186, "Expressions of Beauty".

79: Selection 4: Letter of September 6, 1986.

"*Say* Allāh! *and leave them to their vain discourse*" (Koran, *Sūrah* "Cattle" [6]:92).

Et in terra pax hominibus bonae voluntatis—Latin for "And on earth peace to men of good will" —is from the Gloria of the Roman Catholic Mass.

Selection 5: "The Book of Keys", No. 809, "Possibility and Destiny".

80: Selection 6: "No Activity without Truth", for a congress in Japan, 1961.

For a more extended critique of *anti-traditional culture* see the author's "To Have a Center", in *To Have a Center: A New Translation with Selected Letters*, ed. Harry Oldmeadow, pp. 3-30.

81: Selection 7: Undated letter.

Selection 8: "No Activity without Truth", for a congress in Japan, 1961.

82: Selection 9: Undated letter.

Selection 10: Letter of October 31, 1972.

83: Selection 11: Undated and untitled note.

For *Hamlet* see editor's note for "The Play of Masks", p. 23, Note 2.

"*Vanity of vanities. . . . What profit hath a man of all his labor which he taketh under the sun? . . . The thing that hath been, it is that which shall be; and that which is done is that which shall be done: and there is no new thing under the sun*" (Ecclesiastes 1:2-9).

Selection 12: "The Book of Keys", No. 244, "Concentration and Sovereign Good"

"*I am black, but beautiful*" (Song of Sol. 1:5).

84: Selection 13: "No Activity without Truth", for a congress in Japan, 1961.

85: Selection 14: "The Book of Keys", No. 262, "Spiritual Anthropology".

For *Meister Eckhart* and the saying that "There is something in the soul that is uncreated and uncreatable, and this is the Intellect" see editor's notes for

"Prerogatives of the Human State", p. 7 and "Delineations of Original Sin", p. 50, Note 6.

"*Made in the image of God*": "So God created man in his own image, in the image of God created he him; male and female created he them" (Gen. 1:27).

86: Selection 15: "No Activity without Truth", for a congress in Japan, 1961.

Selection 16: "No Activity without Truth", for a congress in Japan, 1961.

87: For "*the latter days*" see editor's note for "Prerogatives of the Human State", p. 5, Note 3.

88: Selection 17: "The Book of Keys", No. 1059, "O *Beata Certitudo, O Certa Beatitudo*".

"*Love Him with all our faculties*": "Thou shalt love the Lord thy God with all thy heart, and with all thy soul, and with all thy strength, and with all thy mind" (Luke 10:27); "this is the first and great commandment," says Christ (Matt. 22:37; cf. Mark 12:30, Deut. 6:5).

For O *beata certitudo, O certa beatitudo* see editor's note for "Prerogatives of the Human State", p. 12.

89: Selection 18: Undated, untitled note.

Norms and Paradoxes in Initiatic Alchemy

91: For "*dark age*" and *kali-yuga* see editor's note for "Prerogatives of the Human State", p. 5, Note 3.

"*Made in the image of God*": "And God said, Let us make man in our image, after our likeness" (Gen. 1:26).

The *Upanishads*, also referred to as the *Vedānta* since they were traditionally placed at the "end" of the *Vedas*, are Hindu scriptures which contain metaphysical, mystical, and esoteric doctrine.

The *Brahma Sūtras*, one of the chief sources of Vedantic wisdom, traditionally attributed to the sage *Badarayana* (first century B.C.), distills and systematizes the teachings of the *Upanishads* concerning *Brahma*, the Supreme Reality.

For "Brahman *is Reality; the world is appearance; the soul is not other than*

Brahman" see editor's note for "Prerogatives of the Human State", p. 5.

For *Shankara* see editor's note for "Prerogatives of the Human State", p. 7.

Shivaism is a theistic sect of the Hindu religion whose members worship the God Shiva as the supreme Deity.

Ramanuja (1017-c. 1157) was the foremost exponent of *Vishishta Advaita*, the Hindu school of "qualified non-dualism", which emphasizes the personal nature of God.

Vishnuism, or Vaishnavism, is a theistic sect of the Hindu religion whose members worship the God Vishnu as the supreme Deity.

"Rejoice always, *pray without ceasing*, give thanks in all circumstances; for this is the will of God in Christ Jesus for you" (1 Thess. 5:16-18).

92: The "*motionless mover*", or Unmoved Mover, is the classic expression of *Aristotle* for the divine Principle, as in *Metaphysics*, 1072b.

"*Beauty is the splendor of the true*" is an axiom attributed by the author to Plato.

93: "*In the beginning was the Word*, and the Word was with God, and the Word was God" (John 1:1).

96: The *Fedeli d'Amore* ("liegemen of love") were a group of medieval poets, including Dante, who transposed the courtly ideal of love for the earthly beloved—in Dante's case, Beatrice—into a means of deepening one's love for God.

97: For *Ibn Arabi* see editor's note for "Appendix: Selections from Letters", p. 78.

Dante Alighieri's (1265-1321) *Divine Comedy*, one of the summits of world literature, concludes with a celebration of *l'Amor che muove il sole e l'altre stelle*, "the Love that moves the sun and other stars" (*Paradiso*, Canto 33:145).

98: For *Krishna* see editor's note for "Man in the Cosmogonic Projection", p. 17.

GLOSSARY OF FOREIGN TERMS AND PHRASES

Ab extra (Latin): literally, "from outside"; proceeding from something extrinsic or external.

Ab intra (Latin): literally, "from within"; proceeding from something intrinsic or internal.

Advaita (Sanskrit): "non-dualist" interpretation of the *Vedānta*; Hindu doctrine according to which the seeming multiplicity of things is regarded as the product of ignorance, the only true reality being *Brahma*, the One, the Absolute, the Infinite, which is the unchanging ground of appearance.

A fortiori (Latin): literally, "from greater reason"; used when drawing a conclusion inferred to be even stronger than the one already put forward.

Allāh (Arabic): literally, "God"; a term used by both Muslims and Arab Christians to refer to the One God.

Anamnesis (Greek): literally, a "lifting up of the mind"; recollection or remembrance, as in the Platonic doctrine that all knowledge is a recalling of truths latent in the soul.

Ānanda (Sanskrit): "Bliss", "Beatitude", "Joy"; one of the three essential aspects of *Brahma*, together with *Sat*, "Being", and *Chit*, "Consciousness".

Anima (Latin): soul; see *corpus* and *spiritus*.

Apara-Brahma (Sanskrit): the "non-supreme" or penultimate *Brahma*, also called *Brahma saguna*; in Schuon's teaching, the "relative Absolute".

Apocatastasis (Greek): "restitution, restoration"; among certain Christian theologians, including Clement of Alexandria, Origen, and Gregory of Nyssa, the doctrine that all creatures will finally be saved.

A posteriori (Latin): literally, "from after"; subsequently; proceeding from effect to cause or from experience to principle.

A priori (Latin): literally, "from before"; in the first instance; proceeding from cause to effect or from principle to experience.

Ātmā or *Ātman* (Sanskrit): the real or true "Self", underlying the ego and its manifestations; in the perspective of *Advaita Vedānta*, identical with *Brahma*.

Avatāra (Sanskrit): a divine "descent"; the incarnation or manifestation of God, especially of Vishnu in the Hindu tradition.

Avidyā (Sanskrit): "ignorance" of the truth; spiritual delusion, unawareness of *Brahma*.

Barakah (Arabic): "blessing", grace; in Islam, a spiritual influence or energy emanating originally from God, but often attached to sacred objects and spiritual persons.

Bhakta (Sanskrit): a follower of the spiritual path of *bhakti*; a person whose relationship with God is based primarily on adoration and love.

Bhakti or *bhakti-mārga* (Sanskrit): the spiritual "path" (*mārga*) of "love" (*bhakti*) and devotion; see *jnāna* and *karma*.

Bodhi (Sanskrit, Pali): "awakened, enlightened"; in Buddhism, the attainment of perfect clarity of mind, in which things are seen as they truly are.

Brahmā (Sanskrit): God in the aspect of Creator, the first divine "person" of the *Trimūrti*; to be distinguished from *Brahma*, the Supreme Reality.

Brahma or *Brahman* (Sanskrit): the Supreme Reality, the Absolute.

Brahma nirguna (Sanskrit): *Brahma* considered as transcending all "qualities", attributes, or predicates; God as He is in Himself; also called *Para-Brahma*.

Brahma saguna (Sanskrit): *Brahma* "qualified" by attributes and predicates; God insofar as He can be known by man; also called *Apara-Brahma*.

Brahma Sūtras (Sanskrit): a collection of 555 aphorisms and verses, traditionally ascribed to Badarayana, in which the philosophy of *Vedānta* is tersely articulated; also referred to as the *Vedānta Sūtras*.

Buddhi (Sanskrit): "Intellect"; the highest faculty of knowledge, distinct from *manas*, that is, mind or reason.

Chit (Sanskrit): "consciousness"; one of the three essential aspects of *Apara-Brahma*, together with *Sat*, "being", and *Ānanda*, "bliss, beatitude, joy".

Corpus (Latin): body; see *anima* and *spiritus*.

Corruptio optimi pessima (Latin): a scholastic axiom meaning, the "corruption of the best is the worst".

Glossary

Creatio ex nihilo (Latin): literally "creation out of nothing"; a Semitic monotheistic dogma according to which God drew creation out of no pre-existent reality; often set in contrast to emanationist cosmogonies.

Credo ut intelligam (Latin): "I believe so that I may understand."

De facto (Latin): literally, "from the fact"; denoting something that is such "in fact", if not necessarily "by right".

De jure (Latin): literally, "by right"; an expression often used in contradistinction with *de facto*.

Deva (Sanskrit): literally, "shining one"; in Hinduism, a celestial being; any of the gods of the *Veda*s, traditionally reckoned as thirty-three.

Dharma (Sanskrit): in Hinduism, the underlying "law" or "order" of the cosmos as expressed in sacred rites and in actions appropriate to various social relationships and human vocations; moral duty; in Buddhism, the practice and realization of Truth.

Dhikr (Arabic): "remembrance" of God, based upon the repeated invocation of His Name; central to Sufi practice, where the remembrance is often supported by the single word *Allāh*.

Distinguo (Latin): literally, "I mark or set off, differentiate", often used in the dialectic of the medieval scholastics; any philosophical distinction.

Eidos (Greek): "Idea", "Form", "Paradigm"; in Platonic philosophy, the principial archetype or supra-formal model of formal, created things.

Et in terra pax hominibus bonae voluntatis (Latin): "And peace on earth to men of good will" (cf. Luke 2:14).

Fedeli d'Amore (Italian): "the faithful of love"; a group of Medieval poets, including Dante, who transposed the courtly ideal of love for the earthly beloved—in Dante's case, Beatrice—into a means of deepening one's love for God.

Felix culpa (Latin): literally, "O happy fault"; the sin of Adam understood as a hidden blessing since it required the coming of Christ as redeemer.

Gnosis (Greek): "knowledge"; spiritual insight, principial comprehension, divine wisdom.

Gopī (Sanskrit): literally, "keeper of the cows"; in Hindu tradition, one of the cowherd girls involved with Krishna in the love affairs of his youth, symbolic of the soul's devotion to God.

Gott (German): "God"; Being, or the personal Divinity, as distinguished from *Gottheit*, the "Godhead" or supra-personal Divinity.

Gottheit (German): Divinity, Divine Essence, Beyond-Being; the "Godhead" or supra-personal Divinity; distinguished from *Gott* ("God"), Being, or the personal Divinity.

Heyoka (Lakota): in Sioux culture, a "holy fool" or "sacred clown".

Homo sapiens (Latin): literally, "wise man"; the human species.

Imago Dei (Latin): literally, "image of God"; man—both male and female— created in the likeness of God (cf. Gen. 1:27).

Increatum et increabile (Latin): "uncreated and uncreatable"; transcending the domain of time and relativity, as the Absolute or its prolongations.

In divinis (Latin): literally, "in or among divine things"; within the divine Principle; the plural form is used insofar as the Principle comprises both *Para-Brahma*, Beyond-Being or the Absolute, and *Apara-Brahma*, Being or the relative Absolute.

Intelligo ut credam (Latin): "I understand that I may believe".

Ipso facto (Latin): by that very fact.

Īshvara (Sanskrit): literally, "possessing power", hence master; God understood as a personal being, as Creator and Lord; manifest in the *Trimūrti* as Brahmā, Vishnu, and Shiva.

Japa-Yoga (Sanskrit): method of "union" or "unification" (*yoga*) based upon the "repetition" (*japa*) of a *mantra* or sacred formula, often containing one of the Names of God.

Jiriki (Japanese): literally, "power of the self"; a Buddhist term for spiritual methods that emphasize one's own efforts in reaching the goal of liberation or salvation, as for example in Zen; in contrast to *tariki*.

Jivātmā or *jivātman* (Sanskrit): literally, "the living self"; in Hindu tradition, the personal or individual soul associated with the physical body, as distinct from *Ātmā*.

Jīvan-mukta (Sanskrit): one who is "liberated" while still in this "life"; a person who has attained a state of spiritual perfection or self-realization before death; in contrast to *videha-mukta*, one who is liberated at the moment of death; see *krama-mukta*.

Jōdo or *Jōdo-Shinshū* (Japanese): "pure land" or "true pure land school"; a sect of Japanese Buddhism founded by Shinran, based on faith in the power of the Buddha Amida to bring his devotees to his untainted, transcendent realm and characterized by use of the *nembutsu*.

Jnāna or *jnāna-mārga* (Sanskrit): the spiritual "path" (*mārga*) of "knowledge" (*jnāna*) and intellection; see *bhakti* and *karma*.

Jnānī or *Jnānin* (Sanskrit): a follower of the path of *jnāna*; a person whose relationship with God is based primarily on sapiential knowledge or gnosis.

Kali-Yuga (Sanskrit): in Hinduism, the fourth and final *yuga* in a given cycle of time, corresponding to the Iron Age of Western tradition and culminating in a *pralaya* or the *mahāpralaya*; the present age of mankind, distinguished by its increasing disorder, violence, and forgetfulness of God.

Kalpa (Sanskrit): in Hinduism, a "day in the life of Brahmā", understood as lasting one thousand *mahāyugas* or fourteen *manvantaras*.

Karma (Sanskrit): "action, work"; one of the principal *mārgas* or spiritual "paths", characterized by its stress on righteous deeds (see *bhakti* and *jnāna*); in Hinduism and Buddhism, the law of consequence, in which the present is explained by reference to the nature and quality of one's past actions.

Karma-mārga, karma-yoga (Sanskrit): the spiritual "path" (*mārga*) or method of "union" (*yoga*) based upon right "action, work" (*karma*); see *bhakti* and *jnāna*.

Katharsis (Greek): literally, "purification", "cleansing"; in Greek philosophy, the purgation of negative thoughts and emotions in the soul's ascent to knowledge.

Krama-mukta (Sanskrit): one who obtains "deferred" or "gradual liberation"; one who is liberated by intermediate stages through various posthumous states; see *jīvan-mukta*.

Kōan (Japanese): "precedent for public use", case study; in Zen Buddhism, a question or anecdote often based on the experience or sayings of a notable master and involving a paradox or puzzle that cannot be solved in conventional terms or with ordinary thinking.

L'Amor che muove il sole e l'altre stelle (Italian): "the Love that moves the sun and other stars" (Dante, *Paradiso*, Canto 33:145).

Lā ilāha illā 'Llāh (Arabic): "There is no god but God"; see *Shahādah*.

Līlā (Sanskrit): "play, sport"; in Hinduism, the created universe is said to be the result of divine play or playfulness, a product of God's delight and spontaneity.

Logos (Greek): "word, reason"; in Christian theology, the divine, uncreated Word of God (cf. John 1:1); the transcendent Principle of creation and revelation; in its created aspect, the various prophets insofar as they transmit the Word of God to humanity.

Mahāpralaya (Sanskrit): in Hinduism, the "great" or final "dissolving" of the universe at the end of a *kalpa*, or "day in the life of *Brahmā*", understood as lasting one thousand *yuga*s.

Mahāyāna (Sanskrit): "great vehicle"; the form of Buddhism, including such traditions as Zen and *Jōdo-shinshū*, which regards itself as the fullest or most adequate expression of the Buddha's teaching; distinguished by the idea that *nirvāna* is not other than *samsāra* truly seen as it is.

Mahāyuga (Sanskrit): literally, a "great age"; in the Hindu theory of cosmic cycles as derived from the *Mānava-Dharma-Shāstra*, a period of four *yuga*s.

Manas (Sanskrit): the individual mind or inner sense.

Mandala (Sanskrit): "circle"; in Hinduism and Buddhism, a symbolic representation of the universe, used in religious ceremonies and meditation.

Mantra (Sanskrit): "instrument of thought"; a word or phrase of divine origin, often including a Name of God, repeated by those initiated into its proper use as a means of salvation or liberation; see *japa-yoga*.

Manvantara (Sanskrit): in the Hindu theory of cosmic cycles as derived from the *Mānava-Dharma-Shāstra*, a period of seventy-one *mahāyuga*s; see *yuga*.

Māyā (Sanskrit): universal illusion, relativity, appearance; in *Advaita Vedānta*, the veiling or concealment of *Brahma* in the form or under the appearance of a lower, relative reality; also, as "productive power", the unveiling or manifestation of *Ātmā* as "divine art" or theophany. *Māyā* is neither real nor unreal, and ranges from the Supreme Lord to the "last blade of grass".

Glossary

Mea culpa (Latin): literally, "my fault", "my mistake"; deriving from the *Confiteor* prayer in the Latin rite of confession.

Metatron (Hebrew): in Jewish Kabbalah, the Universal Spirit; also characterized as Universal Man and Prince of the Angels.

Moksha (Sanskrit): "release" or "liberation" from *samsāra*; according to Hindu teaching, the most important of the aims of life, attained by following one of the principal *mārgas* or spiritual paths (see *bhakti, jnāna,* and *karma*).

Mūdra (Sanskrit): literally, "seal"; in Hinduism and Buddhism, a symbolical ritual gesture, most often of the hands or fingers.

Mutatis mutandis (Latin): literally, "those things having been changed which need to be changed".

Nembutsu (Japanese): "remembrance or mindfulness of the Buddha", based upon the repeated invocation of his Name.

Nirvāna (Sanskrit): literally, "blowing out" or "extinction"; in Indian traditions, especially Buddhism, the extinction of suffering and the resulting, blissful state of liberation from egoism and attachment; extinction in relation to universal manifestation.

Noblesse oblige (French): literally, "nobility obliges"; the duty of the nobility to display honorable and generous conduct.

O beata certitudo, o certa beatitudo (Latin): "O blessed certitude, O certain beatitude".

O beata solitudo, o sola beatitudo (Latin): "O blessed solitude, O sole beatitude".

Om (Sanskrit): in Hinduism, the sacred monosyllable symbolizing *Brahma* or the Absolute; also prevalent in Buddhism as a mantric syllable.

Om mani padme hum (Sanskrit): "Om, jewel in the lotus, hum"; an invocatory formula, or *mantra*, used extensively in Tibetan Buddhism.

Para-Brahma (Sanskrit): the "supreme" or ultimate *Brahma*, also called *Brahma nirguna*; in Schuon's teaching, the "pure Absolute".

Paramātmā (Sanskrit): the "supreme" or ultimate Self; see *Ātmā*.

Par excellence (French): preeminent; the best of its kind.

Pontifex (Latin): "bridge-maker"; man as the link between heaven and earth.

Prajnā (Sanskrit): "wisdom, intelligence, understanding"; in Hinduism, the self-awareness of *Ātmā*; knowledge of things as they truly are; in Buddhism, the wisdom or truth that complements the spiritual method or way (*upāya*).

Pralaya (Sanskrit): "dissolution"; Hindu teaching that all appearance is subject to a periodic process of destruction and recreation; see *mahāpralaya*.

Princeps hujus mundi (Latin): "prince of this world"; Satan, the devil.

Qua (Latin): "as", "in the capacity of".

Quod absit (Latin): literally, "which is absent from, opposed to, or inconsistent with"; a phrase commonly used by the medieval scholastics to call attention to an idea that is absurdly inconsistent with accepted principles.

Raison d'être (French): "reason for being".

Rūh (Arabic): "breath, spirit"; in the Koran (*Sūrah "Al-Hijr"* [15]:29), the breath breathed into human beings by God to bring them to life.

Sādhana (Sanskrit): spiritual path; in Hinduism, a path typically involving the use of a *mantra* and visualization of the chosen deity.

Samsāra (Sanskrit): literally, "wandering"; in Hinduism and Buddhism, transmigration or the cycle of birth, death, and rebirth; also the world of apparent flux and change.

Sannyāsin (Sanskrit): "renunciate"; in Hindu tradition, one who has renounced all formal ties to social life.

Sat (Sanskrit): "being"; one of the three essential aspects of *Apara-Brahma*, together with *Chit*, "consciousness", and *Ānanda*, "bliss, beatitude, joy".

Satori (Japanese): in Zen Buddhism, the sudden experience of enlightenment; a flash of intuitive insight often gained through the employment of a *kōan* during *zazen* or "sitting meditation"; see *bodhi*.

Shahādah (Arabic): the fundamental "profession" or "testimony" of faith in Islam, consisting of the words *Lā ilāha illā 'Llāh, Muhammadan rasūlu 'Llāh*: "There is no god but God; Muhammad is the messenger of God."

Sophia (Greek): "wisdom"; in Jewish and Christian tradition, the Wisdom of God, often conceived as feminine (cf. Prov. 8).

Glossary

Sophia Perennis (Latin): "perennial wisdom"; the eternal, non-formal Truth at the heart of all orthodox religious traditions.

Spiritus (Latin): Spirit; the supra-individual principle of the human microcosm, with its seat in the heart; see *anima* and *corpus*.

Sūtra (Sanskrit): literally, "thread"; a Hindu or Buddhist sacred text; in Hinduism, any short, aphoristic verse or collection of verses, often elliptical in style; in Buddhism, a collection of the discourses of the Buddha.

Tao (Chinese): literally, "way"; in Taoism, the ultimate Source of all things, from which they come and to which they return; the Way of the universe and the sage.

Tariki (Japanese): literally, "power of the other"; a Buddhist term for forms of spirituality that emphasize the importance of grace or celestial assistance, especially that of the Buddha Amida, as in the Pure Land schools; in contrast to *jiriki*.

Trimūrti (Sanskrit): literally, "having three forms"; in Hindu tradition, a triadic expression of the Divine, especially in the form of Brahmā, the creator, Vishnu, the preserver, and Shiva, the transformer.

Upanishad (Sanskrit): "to sit close by"; hence, any esoteric doctrine requiring direct transmission from master to disciple; in Hinduism, the genre of sacred texts that end or complete the *Veda*s.

Upāya (Sanskrit): "means, expedient, method"; in Buddhist tradition, the adaptation of spiritual teaching to a form suited to the level of one's audience.

Veda (Sanskrit): a body of sacred knowledge revealed to ancient Indian seers and transmitted in the *Veda*s, sacred texts composed of hymns, ritual formulas, and metaphysical doctrines regarded in Hinduism as authoritative for both doctrine and practice.

Vedānta (Sanskrit): "end or culmination of the Vedas"; one of the major schools of traditional Hindu philosophy, based in part on the Upanishads. The three main schools of *Vedānta* are: (1) *Advaita Vedānta* (non-dualism), whose chief representative is Shankara; (2) *Vishishtādvaita Vedānta* (qualified non-dualism), whose chief representative is Ramanuja; and (3) *Dvaita Vedānta* (dualism), whose chief representative is Madhva.

Videha-Mukta (Sanskrit): one who is "liberated" at the moment of death; see *jīvan-mukta*.

Vincit omnia Veritas (Latin): "Truth conquers all".

Vox populi vox Dei (Latin): "the voice of the people is the voice of God".

Yin-Yang (Chinese): in Chinese tradition, two opposite but complementary forces or qualities, from whose interpenetration the universe and all its diverse forms emerge; *yin* corresponds to the feminine, the yielding, the moon, liquidity; *yang* corresponds to the masculine, the resisting, the sun, solidity.

Yoga (Sanskrit): literally, "yoking, union"; in Indian traditions, any meditative and ascetic technique designed to bring the soul and body into a state of concentration.

Yuga (Sanskrit): an "age" in Hinduism, one of the four periods into which a cycle of time is divided.

Zazen (Japanese): literally, "sitting meditation"; in Zen Buddhism, a contemplative practice, often used in conjunction with the *kōan,* and seen as the most direct path to enlightenment.

INDEX

Abraham, 34, 107
Absolute, the, *viii, ix,* 2, 6, 8, 9, 11,
    12, 15, 17, 21, 32, 33, 34, 37,
    39, 41, 42, 43, 44, 63, 64, 67,
    68, 69, 70, 73, 80, 81, 84, 88,
    89, 91, 96, 97, 119, 120, 122,
    125
accident, the, 57, 71, 72
Adam, 10, 31, 50, 101, 103, 106,
    109, 121
alchemy, spiritual, 9, 22, 92
Allāh, 78, 79, 97, 115, 119, 121
All-Possibility, 12, 15, 17, 21, 22,
    25, 29, 31, 32, 37, 97
anamnesis, 95
Ānanda, 38, 93, 119, 120, 126
angels, the, 9, 10, 33, 34, 50, 68,
    109
Anselm, Saint, 67, 113
archangels, the, 33, 50
archetypes, the, 19, 45
Aristotle, 34, 37, 107, 117
Arjuna, 23, 104
atheism, 63
Ātmā, viii, xiii, 7, 17, 18, 22, 26, 32,
    33, 35, 38, 41, 42, 57, 72, 93,
    102, 119, 122, 124, 125, 126
Augustine, Saint, 54, 103, 110
Augustus, emperor, 23
avatāra, 17, 23, 28, 103, 105, 120

barakah, 10
Beautiful, the, *ix,* 1, 97
Beauty, *ix,* 1, 3, 5, 32, 38, 39, 77,
    78, 92, 96, 97, 101, 102, 107,
    114, 115, 117
Being, 1, 11, 13, 15, 16, 19, 20, 21,
    22, 30, 31, 32, 33, 34, 37, 39,
    42, 43, 50, 60, 67, 81, 92, 93,
    96, 97, 113, 119, 122
Bernard, Saint, 12, 102
Beyond-Being, 15, 19, 20, 21, 32,
    33, 34, 42, 122
Bhagavad Gītā, the, 64, 104, 112
bhakti, 6, 58, 120, 123, 125
Blessed Virgin, 27, 105. *See also*
    Mary
Bodhi, 97, 120
Brahma Sūtras, 91, 116, 120
Brahma, Brahman, viii, 7, 19, 32,
    48, 68, 69, 91, 101, 103, 109,
    113, 116, 117, 119, 120, 122,
    124, 125, 126
Buddha, the, 87, 95, 123, 124, 125,
    127
Buddhi, 2, 120
Buddhism, 2, 87, 94, 103, 120, 121,
    123, 124, 125, 126, 127

certitude, 2, 12, 39, 43, 49, 67, 69,
    82, 84, 88, 89, 92, 96, 97, 102,
    125
charity, 3, 4, 6, 9, 21, 22, 24, 25, 53,
    54, 59, 60, 70, 92, 98
Chit, 93, 119, 120, 126
Christ, 28, 33, 56, 58, 68, 69, 103,
    104, 106, 108, 110, 113, 114,
    116, 117, 121. *See also* Jesus
Christianity, 2, 27, 85, 107
concentration, 9, 55, 70, 83, 84, 91,
    94, 95, 96
contemplation, 6, 12, 70, 83, 96
contingency, 26, 27, 29, 30, 31, 32,
    37, 38, 39, 41, 42, 43, 44, 59,

BIOGRAPHICAL NOTES

Frithjof Schuon

Born in Basle, Switzerland in 1907, Frithjof Schuon was the twentieth century's pre-eminent spokesman for the perennialist school of comparative religious thought.

The leitmotif of Schuon's work was foreshadowed in an encounter during his youth with a marabout who had accompanied some members of his Senegalese village to Basle for the purpose of demonstrating their African culture. When Schuon talked with him, the venerable old man drew a circle with radii on the ground and explained: "God is the center; all paths lead to Him." Until his later years Schuon traveled widely, from India and the Middle East to America, experiencing traditional cultures and establishing lifelong friendships with Hindu, Buddhist, Christian, Muslim, and American Indian spiritual leaders.

A philosopher in the tradition of Plato, Shankara, and Eckhart, Schuon was a gifted artist and poet as well as the author of over twenty books on religion, metaphysics, sacred art, and the spiritual path. Describing his first book, *The Transcendent Unity of Religions*, T. S. Eliot wrote, "I have met with no more impressive work in the comparative study of Oriental and Occidental religion", and world-renowned religion scholar Huston Smith said of Schuon, "The man is a living wonder; intellectually apropos religion, equally in depth and breadth, the paragon of our time". Schuon's books have been translated into over a dozen languages and are respected by academic and religious authorities alike.

More than a scholar and writer, Schuon was a spiritual guide for seekers from a wide variety of religions and backgrounds throughout the world. He died in 1998.

Harry Oldmeadow was, until his recent retirement, the Coordinator of Philosophy and Religious Studies at La Trobe University Bendigo, in southeast Australia. A widely respected author on the *sophia perennis* and the perennialist school, his publications include *Traditionalism: Religion in the Light of the Perennial Philosophy* (2000) and *Frithjof Schuon and the Perennial Philosophy* (2010). He has edited several anthologies for World Wisdom, the most recent being *Crossing Religious Frontiers* (2010), and has contributed to such journals as *Sophia* and *Sacred Web*. In addition to his studies of perennialism, he has written extensively on the modern encounter of Eastern and Western traditions in works such as *Journeys East: 20th Century Western Encounters with Eastern Religious Traditions* (2004) and *A Christian Pilgrim in India: The Spiritual Journey of Swami Abhishiktananda* (2008).